Al-Anon's
Twelve
Steps
&
Twelve
Traditions

REVISED

Al-Anon books that may be helpful:

Alateen—Hope for Children of Alcoholics (B-3)

The Dilemma of the Alcoholic Marriage (B-4)

The Al-Anon Family Groups—Classic Edition (B-5)

One Day at a Time in Al-Anon (B-6), Large Print (B-14)

Lois Remembers (B-7)

Alateen—a day at a time (B-10)

As We Understood... (B-11)

...In All Our Affairs: Making Crises Work for You (B-15)

Courage to Change—One Day at a Time in Al-Anon II (B-16), Large Print (B-17)

From Survival to Recovery: Growing Up in an Alcoholic Home (B-21)

How Al-Anon Works for Families & Friends of Alcoholics (B-22)

Courage to Be Me—Living with Alcoholism (B-23)

Paths to Recovery—Al-Anon's Steps, Traditions, and Concepts (B-24)

Living Today in Alateen (B-26)

Hope for Today (B-27), Large Print (B-28)

Al-Anon's
Twelve Steps & Twelve Traditions

REVISED

AL-ANON FAMILY GROUP HEADQUARTERS, INC.
World Service Office for Al-Anon and Alateen
Virginia Beach, Virginia

For information and catalog of literature write to
World Service Office for Al-Anon and Alateen
Al-Anon Family Group Headquarters, Inc.
1600 Corporate Landing Parkway
Virginia Beach, VA 23454-5617
Phone: (757)-563-1600 Fax (757) 563-1655 E-mail wso@al-anon.org
www.al-anon.alateen.org/members

This book is also available in: Danish, Finnish, French, German, Hebrew, Italian, Norwegian, Polish, Portuguese, Spanish, and Swedish.

Al-Anon/Alateen is supported by members' voluntary contributions and from the sale of our Conference Approved Literature.

Library of Congress Catalog Card No. 83-28087
ISBN-978-0-910034-43-2

Publisher's Cataloging in Publication
Al-Anon's twelve steps & twelve traditions.
  p. cm
  Includes index.
  LCCN 83-028087.
  ISBN 0-910034-43-5

  1. Alcoholics—Family relationships. 2. Alcoholics—Rehabilitation. 3. Al-Anon Family Group Headquarters, inc. 4. Alcoholics Anonymous. I. Al-Anon Family Group Headquarters, inc. II. Title: Al-Anon's twelve steps and twelve traditions.

HV5278.A66 1990   362.292'3
                                                            QB192-20146

 Approved by
World Service Conference
Al-Anon Family Groups

The Al-Anon Family Groups are a fellowship of relatives and friends of alcoholics who share their experience, strength, and hope in order to solve their common problems. We believe alcoholism is a family illness and that changed attitudes can aid recovery.

Al-Anon is not allied with any sect, denomination, political entity, organization or institution; does not engage in any controversy; neither endorses nor opposes any cause. There are no dues for membership. Al-Anon is self-supporting through its own voluntary contributions.

Al-Anon has but one purpose: to help families of alcoholics. We do this by practicing the Twelve Steps, by welcoming and giving comfort to families of alcoholics, and by giving understanding and encouragement to the alcoholic.

Suggested Preamble to the Twelve Steps

The Serenity Prayer

God grant me the serenity
To accept the things I cannot change,
Courage to change the things I can,
And wisdom to know the difference.

Al-Anon Declaration

Let It Begin with Me
When anyone, anywhere, reaches out for help,
let the hand of Al-Anon and Alateen always be there,
and—*Let It Begin with Me.*

CONTENTS

Preface   ix

History   xi

Part I — Twelve Steps

An Overview of the Twelve Steps   5

Step One   7

Step Two   13

Step Three   19

Step Four   25

Step Five   31

Step Six   39

Step Seven   45

Step Eight   49

Step Nine   55

Step Ten   61

Step Eleven   67

Step Twelve   73

Part II — Twelve Traditions

An Overview of the Twelve Traditions   83

    Tradition One   85

    Tradition Two   91

    Tradition Three   97

    Tradition Four   101

    Tradition Five   105

    Tradition Six   109

    Tradition Seven   115

    Tradition Eight   119

    Tradition Nine   123

    Tradition Ten   127

    Tradition Eleven   131

    Tradition Twelve   135

Epilogue   139

Twelve Concepts of Service   141

Index   143

PREFACE

Like Alcoholics Anonymous, Al-Anon has three Legacies: recovery, unity, and service. The Twelve Steps describe our Legacy of shared experience in recovery. The Twelve Traditions illustrate our Legacy of unity. Our Legacy of service is found in the Twelve Concepts of Service. All three Legacies are for people whose lives are or have been affected by the alcoholism of a relative or friend. They serve as the foundation of our program and keep us centered on our one purpose, independent of all other procedures, therapies, and organizations.

There is a basic interdependence among the Steps, Traditions, and Concepts of Service. This book focuses on our first two Legacies. Further information about the Twelve Concepts of Service can be found in Al-Anon's pamphlet, *The Concepts—Al-Anon's Best Kept Secret?* (P-57), the "Al-Anon's Twelve Concepts of Service" section of the *Al-Anon/Alateen Service Manual* (P-24/27), and the book *Paths to Recovery* (B-24).

The Twelve Steps of Al-Anon are the heart of the program in which anyone affected by an alcoholic can find a new way of life in the fellowship of the Al-Anon Family Groups. The Twelve Traditions provide a backbone of unity for the fellowship on which individual help depends.

The Twelve Steps and Traditions, although spiritually oriented, are not based on any specific religious discipline. They embrace the philosophies of many faiths and religions as well as non-religious, ethical, and moral thought. The designation "God" does not refer to a particular being, force, or concept, but only to God as each of us understands that term. Anyone can find in this program a serene, fulfilling way of life if they can believe in any Power greater than themselves.

As these Steps and Traditions are studied and applied by the members of our fellowship, many among us discover that their usefulness extends far beyond coping with alcoholism. They become our way of life, capable of helping us at all times and in any situation. How well they serve us depends on how we absorb them and how we use them.

This book includes a description of each Step and Tradition, followed by a reflection and a story. These are merely a few of our shared experiences. There are as many stories as there are Al-Anon members.

HISTORY

As the wives of early Alcoholics Anonymous members came together while their husbands were at meetings, they realized their own need for change. They talked over their own difficulties and helped each other find solutions by applying AA's Twelve Steps to their own lives. These groups were born of a real need for personal sharing about living with an alcoholic.

By 1951, some 87 of these groups and other individuals had asked AA to list them in its directory. Because AA's one purpose is to help alcoholics, these requests were referred to Lois W., the wife of AA's cofounder. She and her friend Anne B., the wife of another AA member, became the cofounders of a fellowship for the families and friends of alcoholics. With the help of other pioneer members, they set about unifying these groups and providing them with guidance and service.

For unity's sake, the groups decided on the name "Al-Anon Family Groups" and adapted AA's Twelve Steps for their own purpose. Only one word was changed.

Although Al-Anon was far too young and inexperienced as a fellowship to have established any Traditions of its own, early members knew that unity depended upon living by certain guidelines. Therefore the AA Traditions, also adapted to fit the needs of Al-Anon, became part of the program.

In the early years, the only source of help for children affected by the drinking of others was attendance at Al-Anon and open AA meetings. At these meetings, they learned about alcoholism and its effects on the family. These young people, however, lacked association with others their own age who understood their particular situations.

In 1957, a high school boy in California felt the need to talk with other teenagers who could identify with his sharing. Out of this need, Al-Anon groups for teenage members were created and called "Alateen." As an integral part of Al-Anon, Alateen members follow the same program.

Al-Anon's
Twelve
Steps
&
Twelve
Traditions

Part I

TWELVE STEPS

SUGGESTED PREAMBLE
TO THE TWELVE STEPS

The Al-Anon Family Groups are a fellowship of relatives and friends of alcoholics who share their experience, strength, and hope in order to solve their common problems. We believe alcoholism is a family illness and that changed attitudes can aid recovery.

Al-Anon is not allied with any sect, denomination, political entity, organization, or institution; does not engage in any controversy; neither endorses nor opposes any cause. There are no dues for membership. Al-Anon is self-supporting through its own voluntary contributions.

Al-Anon has but one purpose: to help families of alcoholics. We do this by practicing the Twelve Steps, by welcoming and giving comfort to families of alcoholics, and by giving understanding and encouragement to the alcoholic.

TWELVE STEPS

1. We admitted we were powerless over alcohol—that our lives had become unmanageable.

2. Came to believe that a Power greater than ourselves could restore us to sanity.

3. Made a decision to turn our will and our lives over to the care of God *as we understood Him.*

4. Made a searching and fearless moral inventory of ourselves.

5. Admitted to God, to ourselves, and to another human being the exact nature of our wrongs.

6. Were entirely ready to have God remove all these defects of character.

7. Humbly asked Him to remove our shortcomings.

8. Made a list of all persons we had harmed, and became willing to make amends to them all.

9. Made direct amends to such people wherever possible, except when to do so would injure them or others.

10. Continued to take personal inventory and when we were wrong promptly admitted it.

11. Sought through prayer and meditation to improve our conscious contact with God *as we understood Him,* praying only for knowledge of His will for us and the power to carry that out.

12. Having had a spiritual awakening as the result of these steps, we tried to carry this message to others, and to practice these principles in all our affairs.

AN OVERVIEW
OF THE
TWELVE STEPS

As we study and apply the Twelve Steps, we see more and more clearly how carefully they were thought out and the skill and precision with which each word was chosen. Written in the past tense, they share the experiences of those who have gone before us and offer us an ongoing guide for recovery today.

The first three Steps suggest that our human resources, such as intelligence, knowledge, strength, and even hope, are not enough to solve our problems. As others have done, we can accept the help of a Power greater than our own to guide our thoughts and actions. These three Steps show us how to bring that Power into our lives in an active, workable partnership.

Steps Four through Seven point the way to overcome the personal faults that have caused so many of our problems.

Steps Eight and Nine offer us a way to make specific corrections to relieve us of our burdens of guilt and confusion. Step Ten asks us to continue the effort begun with Step Four, acknowledging our shortcomings and working constantly to rid ourselves of them.

Step Eleven urges us to continue developing a conscious contact with a Power greater than ourselves through prayer and meditation. Step Twelve suggests we practice these principles in all our affairs and share our spiritual growth with others.

STEP ONE

We admitted we were powerless over alcohol—that
our lives had become unmanageable.

Many of us came to Al-Anon to learn the "secret" of compelling
someone close to us to stop the damaging and degrading over-use
of alcohol. How discouraging it seemed at first to be told there was
nothing we could do to force anyone to seek sobriety. Helpless and
hopeless, we were still not ready to surrender. Yet how encouraging
it was to learn that we were not responsible for the drinking, as so
many of us had feared.

By taking Step One we acknowledged that we had no power to
make another person stop drinking. Threats, pleas, and the determined use of our will were equally futile. Our schemes and threats
succeeded only in causing us physical and emotional exhaustion.
We were powerless; we were asked to admit and believe it if we
wanted to make progress in improving the quality of our lives.

Others among us, having shouldered major responsibilities, may
have found it difficult to let go and to admit powerlessness over
something in our lives that we felt must be changed. We thought of
it as defeat and were determined not to be defeated in what we considered a worthy goal—the sobriety of a family member or friend.

When some of us first turned to Al-Anon for help, we were in no
frame of mind to admit anything but how badly life was treating us.
How difficult it was for us to face the idea that there was an area
in which we were so helpless. By going to Al-Anon meetings and

talking to other members, we reminded ourselves of this day-by-day. It became easier to accept something we knew we could not control. Learning that alcoholism was a disease proved to be a great relief. We realized that arguments were useless against a disease. We concluded that nothing we could do directly would stop an alcoholic's drinking or change another person.

At the same time, there were those of us who came to our first Al-Anon meetings after our loved ones had stopped drinking. In the first glow of sobriety, some were unrealistically certain our lives would now be perfect. For others there were new fears and resentments as the alcoholic sought his or her solutions without us. We, too, had to realize the futility of trying to control. When we found ourselves continuing to try to direct others, we reminded ourselves that we had no power and no right to exercise power over anyone but ourselves.

Once we accepted these facts, we discovered an important and inspiring secret: how to free ourselves from frustration and confusion. We set ourselves on the way to becoming contented, well-adjusted people.

When our eyes, ears, and hearts were opened, we could free ourselves from our rigid determination to have things the way we wanted them. Then we began to grow.

We began this growth when we overcame the impulse to criticize or blame, even when we thought we had reason to do so. We reminded ourselves that we would probably only be making matters worse.

The feelings of release, of yielding or letting go, when we acknowledged that no change in others could be forced, helped to loosen the suffocating grip of our destructive emotions: guilt, fear, self-pity, and resentment. We found, to our surprise, a new feeling of relaxation, as though a weight had been lifted from us.

In Al-Anon we learned to express our emotional detachment from our problems in slogans such as "Live and Let Live" and "Let Go and Let God."

Freed from the obsession with another person, we could focus our attention on ourselves. We looked at how our lives had become unmanageable. How did we change our negative attitudes? How did we find the path to self-awareness? What actions did we take to change ourselves for the better? How and where did we get the help we needed?

Our answers lay in taking the Twelve suggested Steps toward recovery, which had been used successfully by others with similar problems. We began with the cornerstone of them all: Step One.

Some order came out of chaos. It became easier and easier to accept the idea we could take charge of ourselves. Each time we detached we moved forward.

With our admissions that we lacked power over alcohol, that we lacked the ability to direct other people's lives, and that our lives were unmanageable, we became ready to look beyond ourselves for the strength we needed to live a new way of life.

Thinking It Over

It isn't easy to admit defeat, especially if I have tried to handle my problems in my own way. But I know I cannot move forward unless I am willing to stop trying to control others and their compulsions. With the help of my friends in the program, I can reinforce my knowledge of the futility of struggling against another person's drinking or thinking.

I know that those who come in contact with this family disease are affected in their actions and reactions. Yet I also know that I was the one who allowed my life to become troubled and confused. If I can take my eyes off others, I can see those things in me that contributed to the harshness of my life. I can remind myself that progress in my recovery from all the anger and frustration can only begin with what I can bring myself to do. I can only begin my search for serenity when I can free myself from my obsession with others.

A Step One Story

My husband, Pete, left on a Friday morning to go into the city to be interviewed for yet another job. At my urgent pleading, he promised to be home by evening.

I should have known! Another sleepless night watching at the window, wondering what had happened this time. How could I have believed in him when he said he'd be back? No use checking the local bars the way I usually did, I thought to myself—he was surely still in the city.

I had promised our local liquor store man that I'd be around on Saturday morning to cover one of Pete's bounced checks. That happened so often, and every time they called me to take care of it, I did. I started out with a heavy heart.

On the way from our house to the nearby railroad station, there's a six-lane highway. Just as I was about to cross, the light turned red. To my horror, there was Pete on the other side, trying to stagger into all that traffic. My first impulse was to rush over, but I knew how hopeless that would be. In my utter desperation, I closed my eyes and said, "Oh, God! Oh, God!"

When I heard the traffic stop for the changing light, I looked up. Across the highway was a stranger with a firm grip on my husband's arm, steering him safely over. When they got to me, I thanked the man, with my voice shaking.

It was then I realized that this life-and-death crisis had been taken care of—and not by me. I was powerless, but God was not. It was then that I finally understood the meaning of the First Step.

There was still that check to take care of—I had promised. I swore this would be the last time and I meant it. I went into the liquor store, still trembling from that shocking experience. I explained that I would no longer cover Pete's checks. If the store-owner was willing to give him credit, he'd have to collect from Pete. The man agreed and then said, "You know, that husband of yours ought to try AA."

What irony! I told him how I'd been trying for years to get him to go.

"Well," he answered, "maybe you've been trying too hard."

After that day I found a new direction. I was free. That one unforgettable shock had brought me to my senses and showed me that I was actually prolonging the problem by trying to run everything. From then on, it was "hands off."

That decision brought about many changes in our lives, because I learned the true and total purpose of that First Step. My life had become completely chaotic and unmanageable—until I learned of the power I had over my own actions.

STEP TWO

Came to believe that a Power greater than ourselves could restore us to sanity.

Taking Step One brought us face-to-face with the truth: We were not equal to the task of changing any other human being. We needed more than our human experience and intelligence to solve the problems of living—especially of living with an alcoholic, whether still drinking or not.

The Second Step suggested that we were not alone with those problems if we "came to believe" that help was within our reach. The words "came to believe" meant a gradual awakening to the reality of a Higher Power in our lives. This Step brought us a glimmer of hope as we made our first timid moves toward establishing a working relationship with "a Power greater than ourselves." We began to perceive that this Power was ready to help us whenever we were ready to accept its guidance.

What could this Power do for us? It "could restore us to sanity."

This may have come as a shock to those of us who had always imagined it was only the alcoholic who needed to be restored to sanity. The very idea that we might not be sane usually brought heated denial. Whether spouse, parent, child, or friend, many of us came to Al-Anon convinced that all the insanity belonged exclusively to the alcoholic. We were dismayed to learn that we, too, needed to change. Al-Anon's program was centered on us, the friends and family who had been trying so hard to make some sense out of living, or having lived, with an alcoholic.

To admit that we were irrational may have required more humility than most of us had. Yet when we finally faced the fact that it was we who must change or live with continued confusion and unhappiness, we found ourselves better able to accept the idea that humility was a vital tool in getting the healing help we needed. This Step foreshadowed the entire spiritual scope of the Al-Anon program.

When we looked closely at ourselves and recalled what we were apt to say and do in various situations, we discovered that our behavior was often distorted by anger, frustration, and fear. That is why many of us reacted to the alcoholic in irrational, hysterical ways. In other words, our actions had not been sane. It would have been only natural for us to think of self-justifying ways to defend what we did, but we learned that our actions were indefensible.

Our irrational behavior took many forms. What about the husband who left young children with a drinking wife and worried himself sick over what could happen while he was away at work? Or the wife who was so scared of her violent husband that she did nothing to protect herself or her children from his unpredictable behavior? Or anyone who allowed a child to get into an automobile with a drinking parent at the wheel?

Consider also those of us who did everything we could to protect alcoholic loved ones from the consequences of drinking. We hid the addiction from relatives and friends, lied to employers, pleaded with judges, and even tried to carry the drinker to a comfortable bed so he or she wouldn't have to face having passed out on the floor the night before! Some of us were so confused, we thought drinking with the alcoholic would leave that much less for them to drink!

Sometimes actions of this kind were motivated by good intentions. More often they were fueled by rage and disappointment. There was almost always an underlying idea that something just might make the alcoholic stop drinking. All we had to do, we imagined, was to figure what that "something" was. Even that attitude was far from sane, we learned. Upon reflection, we had to decide whether our thoughts, words, and actions were those of well-balanced, reasonable people. If we realized they were not, then we looked for help—the kind of spiritual help to be found in Al-Anon.

Once we learned to see our situation as it really was, we understood why it was necessary for us to turn to a Power greater than ourselves. At that point in our Al-Anon experience, it might have been too soon to expect total trust in a Higher Power, especially since we thought we were self-reliant. We might have rejected the idea of a Power greater than ourselves, or once believed in God, but never maintained spiritual contact. We might have thought of this Higher Power only as a punishing God. Those of us brought up in a religious faith may have prayed for something to change the drinker into a normal, responsible human being.

At first some of us could only admit we were powerless to control the events of our lives. With the help and support of Al-Anon, trust in a "Power greater than ourselves" often came in time. That meant being allied to an unfailing source of security and comfort.

Though we may have had setbacks and disappointments, we learned to see these as stages in our growth and as opportunities to learn something we needed to know. They gave us a new perspective and prepared us for solutions we couldn't have foreseen. With calm poise, we accepted disappointments, often unrelated to alcoholism, and saved wear and tear on our nerves. This also demonstrated our confidence that things would ultimately work out as they were meant to be. This was by no means weak resignation, but intelligent recognition of the fact that life held experiences for us—some welcome, some not—but all of them offering insights.

As newcomers deep in despair, we may have come to Al-Anon already determined to make a radical change in our lives, such as court action, separation, or divorce. Other Al-Anon members who had been at this crossroad shared their experiences and pointed out that there might be other options available. As Al-Anon members, we never advised each other to take or not to take action. This was especially true for newcomers, who had not yet absorbed enough Al-Anon ideas to know they had other choices. We found that if we gave a member advice about what action to take, we were making unwarranted judgments and decisions that affected the lives of others. We could, however, share our own experiences and offer a measure of objectivity. Our detachment often led others to make reasoned decisions, rather than emotional ones. In helping ourselves, we helped others to be restored to sanity. Then they were better able to make their own decisions.

Thinking It Over

If I declare that "I came to believe," it means my thinking is already moving forward from Step One, in which I admitted I was powerless.

I have come to believe there is a way for me to bring order into my confused life. These Steps will help me as I move on from one to the next.

Now in Step Two, I am acknowledging there is a Power greater than I am. I know that my human will and wisdom are limited.

There is so much I do not know about myself or others—even those who are close to me. There are things I may never know.

If my words and actions are prompted only by my own impulses, some of which may be negative, they can have troublesome consequences for me. When I have at last realized that my problems are too big to solve by myself, then comes the bright, reassuring thought that I need not be alone with them, if I am willing to accept help from a Higher Power.

A Step Two Story

For my first three years in Al-Anon, I had trouble with the Second Step. In spite of disclaimers in our literature and from members of the groups I attended, it seemed to me there was an effort to make me believe in a narrow, religious interpretation of these Steps. I had not lost my belief in a Power greater than myself, but I came from a background of generations of dissenters from orthodoxy. I wondered if to become a good Al-Anon member, it was necessary for me to believe in a God. Most of the time I kept my mouth shut, but I did a lot of troubled thinking about the theological implications of the Second Step. At a meeting, a longtime member said what I needed to hear to make me comfortable with the Steps in Al-Anon that mention a Higher Power or "God *as we understood Him.*"

"Why worry about interpretations?" she said. "I have come to believe that Al-Anon puts me in touch with the help I need to live a saner and more peaceful life. Why trouble myself in trying to define the power that I know is there? We 'came to believe that a Power greater than ourselves could restore us to sanity.' Let's keep it simple. The Steps are not commandments. They are a set of principles that can bring about a spiritual awakening. They describe shared experiences. As long as I share in these experiences, I don't need to let words or interpretations get in my way."

Because it is so important for me to find my own way, I have also tried to respect other people's beliefs or doubts. I simply share my own strengths without trying to impose my beliefs on others. We are all equals, but we are not all the same.

STEP THREE

Made a decision to turn our will and our lives over
to the care of God **as we understood Him.**

Rarely has a complete pattern for living been compressed into so few words. It grows naturally out of Steps One and Two. First we acknowledged that we had been unable to manage our lives. Next we accepted the idea that our help came from a Power greater than ourselves. Then we made a decision to place our lives in the care of that Power. It was, perhaps, the most important decision we ever made, carrying with it a compelling need to keep aware of it always. Once we made that decision and kept reminding ourselves of it, our Higher Power became a part of our daily lives.

Accepting the Third Step was a discipline we set for ourselves. It took vigilance not to slip and take back the reins into our own hands. We had been trying to solve our problems, make choices, and determine our actions by means of our fallible human wisdom and willpower alone. It was not enough; our failures and disappointments proved this. When we made plans, we realized we couldn't possibly take every contingency into account. This explains why we were often frustrated by failure. We had many changes to make, and we began by learning how to use the help of a Higher Power.

Making this decision to put ourselves in the care of a Higher Power took courage. Above all, it took confidence. It served us well when, day after day, we kept alert to what we were thinking, saying, and doing. It helped to form the habit of including our Higher

Power in our thoughts whenever we had a decision to make. When we thought of it as a daily or even hourly undertaking, it was amazing how readily we acquired the habit.

Every time we consciously reminded ourselves of this Step and followed through on it, we experienced a feeling of achievement and growth. Many a longtime Al-Anon member had the thrilling experience of seeing changes take place in newcomers as they gradually shed their despair and, week-by-week, grew in confidence and understanding.

Then we were ready for the next phrase of Step Three's wonderfully compact plan for living: "to turn our will and our lives over . . ." This will of ours grew out of our personality, experience, beliefs, and habits, which even the most earnest and determined could not change overnight. It was the quality that made us sure we were right. It tempted us to justify what we did and closed our minds to the possibility we might be mistaken. Without spiritual underpinnings, we found ourselves hard-pressed to overcome the drive of a strong will. Such a will, set on a fixed goal, could have defeat built right into it. We might have gotten what we were after, but in the end our triumph would turn into frustration.

All this also applied to the "turning over" of our lives. Day-by-day we functioned more or less automatically. We dealt with the present moment—the current crisis—in the accustomed way, rarely stopping to think whether there was a better way. Yet we liked to think we had control over our lives and we expected our decisions to turn out well. We had only to look back on our many disappointments to realize that our control was at best rare, and more often an illusion.

Where could we look for the help we expected when we turned over "our will and our lives?" Obviously there was no person or address we could go to for the answers we sought. This might have been our first realization that a benign Power was at hand, ready to guide us when we were ready. This was a spiritual gift, an opportunity to be helped, not only when we knew we could not help ourselves, but even when we imagined we could. Our part in this relationship was to learn to recognize, reach out, accept, and act with the inner awareness of the spiritual presence whose direction we decided to follow when we made a decision to turn over our will and our lives.

What did we have to lose by making this decision? Only our stubborn determination to have things our way, or the despair that came from repeated disappointments. What did we have to gain? A new life with purpose, meaning, constant progress, and all the contentment and fulfillment that comes from such growth.

We came then to the closing words of this Third Step: *"...as we understood Him."* It was left entirely up to us what the name God meant to us personally. We might have imagined God to be a ruler and judge, dealing out rewards and punishments. The God of our understanding might have been the quality of Universal Love, revealing itself in our lives. To some it might have been a personal God—powerful but separate from us. Others might have thought of God as an essential part of all creativity.

The God of our understanding was not filtered through any group and not limited to any teaching. Our understanding grew as we developed spiritually through working these Steps. The choice was ours alone. The opportunity to use Divine guidance was given to each of us to interpret and use as we wished.

Thinking It Over

All the experience of my life, my patterns of thought, and my atti-tude are so much a part of me that everything I think, say, and do has become an automatic reaction to what happens outside of me.

Step Three suggests I teach myself, from this moment on, to be receptive. I can open myself to help from my Higher Power. It is a help that may come in many forms, often through other people. I will keep in mind that this relationship I have with God does not mean merely asking for help, but knowing it is there and accepting it.

It's as though I were standing on the shore of a river while my children were on the opposite side, hungry, cold, and frightened. There is a boat at hand, with warm blankets, clothing, and food. Would I just stand there, imploring God to save my children, when I have already been provided with everything I need? No, I'd get into the boat and row across, wrap up the children warmly, feed them, and thank God for knowing my need.

So it is with other problems I may have. Until I have established a relationship with a Higher Power, I may miss many of the obvious solutions to my difficulties.

A Step Three Story

Except for a rare visit to a nearby city, I had never been away from my hometown. I married young, had six children, and then sepa-rated from my alcoholic husband. In Al-Anon I was slow to grasp the program, but as each bit of it sank in, I grew in confidence.

My oldest daughter, then 19, joined the Navy and was sent to a midwestern training station. Things seemed to be going pretty well with her when suddenly I had a call from her training base. She was in the hospital because of an emotional breakdown. I nearly panicked, but I'd really learned to ask for guidance and that was the first thing I did. One thing I knew—I had to get to my child. But how? I had no money. I'd never traveled and I didn't know how to go about getting around in new places. Again and again I almost lost touch with God. I forced myself to keep in mind that He would help me find the way.

I borrowed money for the plane to the nearest big city. From there I knew I'd find some way to get to the Navy base after I arrived. I called our Al-Anon group secretary and she rushed over with the Al-Anon World Directory.* In it I found two names and telephone numbers of members near the base.

When the plane landed, I had just one thought—make a contact with Al-Anon. The first person I called was Barbara. I told her my story and asked her how to get to the base. She told me where to get a bus to the nearest town where she'd be waiting for me.

I don't know how we recognized each other, but Barbara was there to meet me and drove me the ten miles to the base hospital. As we talked on the way, she said: "You mentioned finding a place to stay. You won't need one. We have an extra room, and that will make it handy for driving you to the hospital to see your girl."

I was so overwhelmed that I cried. I knew it wasn't just two strangers meeting. It was two Al-Anon members living with a Higher Power who had taken charge of this crisis.

My daughter was so relieved to see me that she soon showed signs of improvement. Barbara drove me over there every day for a week and made me feel at home. Every time I spoke of how grateful I was to her, she'd say, "Don't you think this is doing just as much for me?"

---

*The World Directory has been replaced by Al-Anon's toll-free meeting line, 1-888-4AL-ANON.

She even drove me all the way to my homebound plane, a distance of over 50 miles. I went with a lightened heart, for the doctor had assured me that my daughter would soon be well enough to return to duty.

This, to me, was Step Three at work. I didn't know where I was going, how I'd get there, or where I'd stay, only that it was all in God's hands.

STEP FOUR

Made a searching and fearless moral inventory of ourselves.

The process of our personal improvement began with Step Four, in which we tackled the work of getting to know ourselves as we really were. Maybe we'd been so preoccupied with thinking about what others were doing, especially the alcoholic, that we never realized how much our own actions needed examining. It was inspiring to realize that we had the ability to become more confident, competent, and mature. Self-discovery was a satisfying goal to look forward to and well worth every bit of effort we put into it. We tried to remember that this was not a single-handed, personal effort—we asked for and accepted the help of a Higher Power every step of the way. We no longer wanted to work alone.

Step Four was a tool for bringing to light the true source of our problems. As we dug deeper to discover just how our own shortcomings had frustrated us, we began to see what we wanted changed in us, not in anybody else. We gradually learned how many of our difficulties were of our own making and could not be blamed on fate, bad luck, or the selfishness and stubbornness of other people.

We took an *inventory*. That's a word usually applied to tangible things: so many chairs, coats, rugs, and other possessions. That kind of inventory is easy enough; they are things we can see and touch. The Step Four inventory, however, was made up of our personal characteristics as we understood and evaluated them. That evaluation was naturally colored by our attitudes, our personal experience, and how honest we could be in recognizing them.

All of us had some qualities we liked, some we didn't, and some of which we were not even aware. Our good qualities gave us strong support in facing the ones that gave us trouble. We may have been tempted to excuse some of our faults because we felt others had treated us badly. Some we may have justified by thinking, "Everybody does that." But the sole purpose of the "searching and fearless moral inventory" was to shed light on what was preventing us from achieving fulfillment.

We began the process of improving as soon as we uncovered the various personal qualities that made us the way we were. Above all, we found it important to get a clear picture of our attitudes and actions toward our family members, relatives, friends, and others. It wasn't easy. Long-established habits were hard to recognize and even harder to change. For many of us, Step Four was a challenge almost too formidable to face. It seemed easier to hide and continue to deny the unpleasant and painful truths. This is understandable; it isn't easy to evaluate deep-rooted attitudes and habits. Many found it helpful to do a written inventory, while others wrote their life story. When we recorded significant events in our lives and honestly wrote how we felt about them, we often discovered that having lived with an alcoholic had not caused our defects. We may have already had shortcomings that would have caused us trouble under any circumstances. Regardless of their origin, we realized that they were *our* defects, and it was now our responsibility to own up to them.

It was important not to condemn ourselves for whatever negative qualities we uncovered in this self-study. Most of us were already burdened with feelings of guilt. Many of us wondered whether we might have been responsible for the alcoholic's drinking, before we learned in Al-Anon that alcoholism is a disease we could not have prevented. Blaming ourselves was not a productive way to improve.

A great lift came as we realized that we were not alone in this undertaking. The guidance and support of our Higher Power was always at hand, reinforced by understanding and loving friends in our Al-Anon group. It was only our own improvement we were striving for—our own flaws we wanted to remove. Measuring our shortcomings by comparing them to those of others only hampered our search for self-understanding. Thus a searching and fearless inventory meant no sidestepping. The inventory in which we listed our character flaws was only a starting point. The main advantage of such a list was that it showed us how to contrast our undesirable characteristics with the good ones that offset them.

Recognizing and acknowledging some of our shortcomings wasn't easy, but it was important. Then too, it was to be a "moral" inventory, one dealing directly with the distinction between what was right and wrong in our conduct. Because each of us had developed our own code of ethics, we took this into account in making our own "moral" inventories. We examined our behavior as it affected us and other people in our lives—especially those close to us.

Thinking It Over

Many of my own shortcomings may be due to confusion, fear, or uneasiness. When I find I am impatient and unreasonable, it is perhaps because I have taken on more than I can handle. Am I under such pressure that I can't even recognize how badly I'm reacting?

Looking for the causes, I might find I have too much to do in a given time period. Maybe I've allowed friends to interrupt my work. I may have been faced with a dreaded obligation or dilemma to be solved. Once I have determined the cause, I can set about getting rid of my impatience and unreasonableness.

In the same way, I can ultimately cope with self-righteousness and intolerance. Perhaps I'm afraid to accept ideas other than those I have lived with for so long. It may be hard for me to see social and political changes without feeling "the old ways were better." When self-pity rears its ugly head, I know I am overlooking many blessings in my life for which I can be grateful.

Surely I can work out the causes of the flaws I acknowledge in my list. I am determined to concentrate on the reasons why I act the way I do in various situations and then try to eliminate the underlying causes.

I know it can be a big help for me to cultivate awareness of people. I will listen to what they are saying, observe their actions, accept them, and do my best to understand.

A Step Four Story

When I first came to Al-Anon my life was crumbling around me. My marriage was breaking up, my house had to be sold, and my two young children and I had nowhere to live. I came to my first meeting and heard the words "lives had become unmanageable" and "restore us to sanity," and I grabbed onto the program like a lifeline. I used the slogans, prayers, and literature to rebuild my life. When the dust settled, I had come through the upheaval with my serenity intact. It had not been painless, but manageable. I didn't even think twice about Step Three. I had made such a mess of things and had found my Higher Power so dependable that I was eager to turn my will and my life over to the God of my understanding.

Then I found myself facing Step Four. I was afraid. I knew I had deep issues that went beyond my husband's alcoholism. I was familiar with a long list of my faults. I was often overwhelmed with feelings of guilt as I began to realize my part in the collapse of my marriage. But the program had given me so much already, and I had heard, "It works if you work it," so often that I got a Sponsor and began my inventory.

I spent several months approaching Step Four from several different angles. I used my *Paths to Recovery* book. I made a resentment list and a list of my part, good and bad, in the key events of my life. What began as a painful experience became a liberating one. When I was done, I had a balanced list of my virtues and faults. I also had a much greater respect for what I had done with my life. But best of all, I had a tool I could use to keep from committing the same errors in judgment that had caused me so much trouble in the past.

For example, while I was usually scrupulously honest, I found I often lied to avoid confrontation. I saw how much trouble lying to avoid confrontation had caused in my life and the lives of others. Sometimes I still feel like responding that way but now I notice it and view each time as an opportunity for change. Little by little, I'm building new habits that keep my life manageable.

I knew when I did my Fourth Step that it wasn't perfect. There were issues I wasn't willing or able to look at right then, but with the support of my group I realized that was fine. Now while I'm working on what I can, I'm also looking forward to a time when I'm ready to face new issues. I know my Higher Power will provide the strength and the opportunity when I'm ready.

STEP FIVE

Admitted to God, to ourselves, and to another human being the exact nature of our wrongs.

Humility is one of the underlying thoughts of the Twelve Steps. Step One sets up the pattern for us: ". . . admitted we were powerless." In Step Two, we acknowledged a "Power greater than ourselves." With Step Three, we relinquished control by deciding to "turn our will and our lives over" to that Power. In Step Four, we faced up to our shortcomings. All of this concerned the quality and purpose of *humility*.

The Step before this one started us on a continuing process of uncovering what we were really like. We learned day by day to observe what actions might have kept us from realizing our true potential and getting from life the serenity it could bring. We decided to do a three-fold "admitting" to God, to ourselves, and to another person.

Admitting to God—first—prepared us for the two things we had to do next: admit our shortcomings to ourselves and to another human being.

It was not a matter of informing our Higher Power of something only we knew. It was rather the effect on *us* of feeling that we could speak to our God without embarrassment or shame. This provided us with a solid base for a clear understanding of ourselves. It was this intimate communication with a Higher Power that made us feel all the more free to bring out everything that needed to come to light—the *exact nature* of our wrongs.

Our method of communicating depended on our personal view and our relationship to the God of our understanding. Some of us might speak to that Power greater than ourselves in thought, perhaps visualizing a kind, understanding presence or Universal Spirit. No matter how we chose to communicate with a Higher Power, it was essential for us to experience the feeling of surrender of our will. This would prepare us for unquestioning acceptance of this guidance in the days and years to come.

Step Five next asked us to admit our shortcomings to ourselves. This might not have been easy, even after we had opened our hearts to a spiritual Power. It was helpful to check our Step Four list for such character flaws as arrogance, self-justification, and resentment, for these three traits may have concealed other faults. Strict honesty and courage helped us with this added effort. We might not have liked what we found, but once we had admitted our imperfections to ourselves, the improving process began.

We might have been tempted to justify our hostile or indifferent feelings about others or to overlook whatever we found too painful to admit. Such evasion would have surely hindered our progress. If we were really trying to isolate our major faults, we found it helpful to observe them in the way we reacted to the people in our daily lives. Such awareness could give us a clearer understanding of the causes of our failures and frustrations.

It was a good idea to undertake these self-examinations when we had been annoyed or hurt by what somebody else had done. We may have wondered why things worked out the way they did, only to find it was our own attitude or action that created the unwelcome result. When we were not at fault, we learned about ourselves by becoming aware of our reactions and discovering what sort of situations had the power to hurt us.

When we reviewed the list of faults we made for Step Four, we found each of these related to some habit, some way we thought, acted, worked, or spoke. If we were quick to resent or to imagine that others were purposely hurtful, we might have uncovered the reasons behind these thoughts by recalling actual instances in which this resentment made problems for us. If our resentment was due to unfulfilled expectations, then we could learn not to expect others to behave exactly as we wanted. If we resented what we regarded as a deliberate unkindness, we asked ourselves whom we were really hurting by feeling bitter. Then we realized we were hurting only ourselves and not the person we resented.

The same thinking-through could be applied to other flaws we discovered. As we learned to understand why we reacted the way we did, we were ready for the next part of the Step and we shared the exact nature of our shortcomings with another person.

Choosing a helpful, understanding Al-Anon member—someone who was really living the program—was a good idea. Usually we did not choose a family member or a close relative— or the alcoholic. Before we decided on confiding in someone outside the fellowship, we took into account that trustworthiness was not the sole consideration. It was also important for our confidant to have knowledge of the program and the purpose of this Step.

Once we had decided on a dependable person, we tried to make our communication as open and honest as possible. There was much more to this than just presenting a list of our shortcomings. We shared frank and detailed explanations: how we felt about these faults, and what we believed to be their exact nature. We found this easier if we were able to avoid feelings of guilt. After all, the faults we described were those we did not even recognize before we began our effort at self-awareness. We made every effort to refrain from passing judgment on ourselves or on others.

In bringing our hidden thoughts about ourselves to another person, we were asking for more than just to be heard. We were also ready to listen to the other person's response to what we had told them. Their experience might not have been the same as ours. The interchange could be productive and helpful only if we were willing to listen with an open mind to someone else's view. We were broadened by accepting ideas that could change us for the better.

No matter how difficult we found this part of Step Five, it brought a tremendous sense of relief. It lightened our own burden to share it with another for whom it was not a burden, but an opportunity to help.

Thinking It Over

It is very comforting to know I can have a personal relationship with a Higher Power of my own choosing. Because God and I have an understanding, I am free to bring my shortcomings to this spiritual friend.

When I admit my imperfections to myself, I give myself a chance to make room for new attitudes and directions. My willingness to look beyond my defensive view and my real or imagined hurts gives me release from carrying them around. If I can search them out and look at them, I can let them go.

Learning to trust and confide in another person means ridding myself of the prejudices I'd acquired with the disease of alcoholism. I can receive a special bonus in establishing this kind of rapport with an Al-Anon Sponsor, who is able to share the recovery tools of the program when I share my feelings. I can use what I have learned to sponsor others. My Sponsor listened—just lis-

tened. *What relief it gives me to unburden myself and what a sense of freedom I feel. I will learn to share my experiences without suggesting solutions for others.*

A Step Five Story

When I took the Twelve Steps for the first time, I ran into quite a few problems. It wasn't until I reached Step Five that I began to uncover some of my most negative characteristics, although I hadn't realized what they were doing to me.

Sure, I'd made a list as Step Four had told me to do. It was as honest as I could make it, but even so, it wasn't much of a list. One of the shortcomings I admitted was procrastination. I just couldn't seem to get things done that needed doing. I had several excuses: I had too much to do; I had been interrupted by others; or the days just weren't long enough. It didn't dawn on me that I was too busy minding other people's business, too busy taking charge of everything and everybody in the family, to take charge of myself.

That's how it went with my whole inventory. I'd put down a flaw and then immediately excuse it. Everything that was wrong with me seemed to be caused by the way other people failed to live up to my expectations. I felt pretty good about myself when I'd finished Step Four. It seemed to prove what I'd always known—that life had dealt me a pretty bad hand! Poor me! Apparently I forgot to include self-pity on my list! I just couldn't see that my own attitude had anything to do with my frustrations.

I marched confidently on to Step Five, certain that what I had to admit to God and to myself wasn't a half-bad record. But as for admitting to another person what was wrong with me, forget it! I didn't know anybody I trusted enough. Besides, I had no intention of laying myself open to criticism.

When the thought struck me, it brought me up short. It was like a sudden light in a dark room. Why was I so suspicious of other people? Why was I so afraid to see myself through someone else's eyes? Was that some kind of shortcoming in me? As these questions came springing into my mind, I began to have misgivings about how honest I'd been in my Fourth Step inventory. And here was the Fifth Step saying to me, "Watch what you are doing! Notice how you react to people. Listen to your own words—to the sound of your own voice. What makes you feel so sorry for yourself? Why don't you listen?"

I made up my mind to complete the part of Step Five I had shied away from—admitting to another human being what I'd found troublesome in me. I realized I couldn't handle this job all by myself as I'd planned to do. That insight helped me swallow my pride and decide to ask someone else to help me. But who? I suddenly realized I had hardly any friends—not even a close association with anyone in my group. It was a real problem, but when I really needed help and admitted my need, help was at hand. I thought of my first Sponsor in my early Al-Anon days who had been so patient with me. After a few months in the program, I figured I knew more about it than anybody, so I gave up having a Sponsor. I realize today that I know less now, after six years in Al-Anon, than I thought I did then.

I called my Sponsor, who was delighted to hear from me and agreed at once to work with me on the self-examination Steps.

It would take too long to tell you the many ways in which this helped change my thinking. It took lots of patience and understanding, because I was a stubborn subject. Eventually I could actually feel the changes taking place in me. I became willing, humbly willing, to turn to my Higher Power for help whenever I needed it. I gained a growing confidence by dealing with my problems. The way other people seemed to accept me and even like me—that was a revelation! Most important, my love for others kept growing.

STEP SIX

Were entirely ready to have God remove all these defects of character.

The purpose of Step Six was to make ourselves ready to accept God's help and to know, with absolute certainty, when we had done so. Taking this Step continued to remind us that we needed the help of a Power greater than ourselves. This ever-available help, however, in no way relieved us of our responsibility to uncover and examine our defects.

We knew these defects might have their roots in deeply-ingrained patterns of behavior that were very much a part of us. What was harder to see and accept was that we were often as comfortable with these defects as with a pair of old shoes. A new pair of shoes takes time to break in. Likewise, the new self we were striving for may have pinched while we were adjusting to it, but we were the only ones who could bring about changes that could mean a new way of life for ourselves. We could not forget we were dependent on a Power greater than ourselves if we really wanted to make a success of this undertaking. It was as though we were going on a journey to an unknown destination. We were eager to get there, but we could not find the way alone. So we reached out for the hand of the guide who pointed out the path we were to follow. Still it was *we* who must do the traveling.

We may have imagined—maybe even with a feeling of hopeless-ness—that we were expected to achieve personal perfection. The

Twelve Steps may seem to ask us to strive for a kind of impossible freedom from all faults. Not so! We came to believe that their real purpose is to show us we have unlimited potential for solving the problems of living. They tell us we can remove the roadblocks—often self-created—that make it so laborious to achieve confidence and peace of mind. When we were first faced with a crisis, we may have examined it from all angles, desperately searching for a solution. We could see no way out, and we knew it was a problem nobody else could solve. But if we were able to open ourselves in total surrender to our Higher Power, inspiration seemed to come from within us to free us from doubt and despair, providing secure confidence that the right answers would come. There, as at every Step, we realized how essential it was to refer all our problems and all our shortcomings to that Higher Power.

When we clung to old habits and to unproductive ways of thinking, we blocked the process of change and the flow of inspiration. The surest way to use God's help was to allow solutions to come to us.

We might have wondered why we held on to our defects. Often they were developed as defenses—and they worked for us. Pride, for instance, allowed us to feel superior, indifferent to our common humanity and its responsibilities. Manipulating the lives of others gave us a feeling of being "in charge." As we learned to accept ourselves and love ourselves, the need for these defenses melted away.

Step Four helped us to uncover our defects of character. With Step Five we faced them courageously and shared them with another human being. We have acknowledged our shortcomings without guilt, or even regret, for we have learned that to blame and punish ourselves would not help us to grow. The guilt feelings were natural, but clinging to them kept us at a standstill.

We may have felt that this process of bringing about fundamental changes in ourselves was too demanding—even overwhelming. It might have been, but the fact that we turned to Al-Anon for help and began studying the Twelve Steps implied our dedication to resolve the troubles that made life so perplexing. Faith in our ability to follow through relieved us of anxiety and made it possible to face and solve, with spiritual wisdom, the problems of each day.

Were we then "entirely ready" to have our faults removed? Surely we wanted a new image of ourselves. We knew there was a radiant, confident personality in each of us, hidden under a mass of confusion, uncertainty, and discontent. If someone were to ask if we wanted to be freed from these hindrances, there could be only one answer—that we were entirely ready to have God remove them.

Thinking It Over

Today I will not cling to the old, worn-out image of myself. I promise to carry in my thoughts the person I'd like to be. One way to do this is to keep alert to the ideas that come automatically to mind, carefully consider the actions and words they suggest to me, and keep myself from acting on impulse.

A sudden spurt of temper can lead me to say hurtful things—often things I do not really mean. This accomplishes nothing—neither for me nor for the person to whom I reacted. Let me think before I speak, unless the impulse that prompts my words is courteous and loving.

Do I really want to continue criticizing and giving advice? Can I be sure my views are right? Has it ever occurred to me that I, too, do many things that my family and friends might find unkind or unfair?

Have I added to my life the little niceties that make it so much more interesting—learning a new skill, having a hobby, or taking time to improve my health and the way I look, walk, talk, and generally appear to others? Am I learning that life does not need to be as dull as I have allowed mine to become?

While I may be proud of the way I deal with people outside our home, do I always treat the members of my own family with respect and courtesy? Aren't there many times in the course of the day when I can give them proof of my acceptance and love? Am I really ready to give up my longtime habit of blaming others for everything that goes wrong?

Do I realize it if I do too much talking? Do I let anyone else be heard? Do I constantly interrupt and take control of a conversation? I might find I could enjoy listening. Perhaps I will learn a new idea or find a fresh point of view.

The faults I carry with me certainly influence the quality of life around me. They can be removed once I make myself entirely ready for this Step and the one that follows it.

A Step Six Story

I already knew from the previous Steps that my biggest problem was really *me* and how I reacted to the events and people in my life. If I continued reacting the way I had always done in the past, I would stay emotionally and spiritually stuck. I recognized these character traits by listening to my words—one day at a time—as they expressed my thoughts and attitudes. I no longer wanted to wallow in self-pity, resentment, anger, and depression.

Working Step Six reminds me of my experience with fingernail biting. Because of my constant worry and nervousness, I often bit my fingernails until they bled. It seemed I had bandages on one finger or another at all times. For years, nail biting was such a habit that I didn't know I was even doing it unless someone pointed it out. I felt ashamed of how my hands looked, but was seemingly powerless over doing anything about it. How could I quit? In spite of all my attempts, I kept automatically biting my nails until these words of the Sixth Step hit home: "Entirely ready." This habit had to go. It did nothing for my self-esteem and I became entirely ready to stop biting one fingernail at a time. I really *did* have the power to change this habit and it began with just being ready and willing to do something a day at a time. Although it took almost a year, I now have ten recovering fingernails!

Like biting my fingernails, my character defects had become unconscious habits. I could no longer blame the alcoholic for my resentment, self-righteousness, sarcasm, anger, overreacting, jealousy, envy, self-pity, and all those other character traits I discovered in my Fourth Step inventory. These were the things separating me from myself, my relationships, and my God. They not only were part of who I had become as a result of living with active alcoholism, but they also were a part of who I was long before I met and married an alcoholic. My Fourth Step inventory became my foundation and reference to continue with Step Six.

Now that I was aware of the things that were causing me trouble, I could continue to identify them as they occurred and immediately ask for help. I couldn't remove them by myself. They had lodged themselves deep in my personality and needed some prying to get out! Sometimes I needed to talk over a situation with my Sponsor to get a different perspective of my problem.

If I want God to grant me the serenity I ask for in the Serenity Prayer, then I need to become entirely ready and willing to change the things I can without criticism or blame. The more I become willing to focus on my own shortcomings and to walk the spiritual way of Al-Anon, the more God helps me move on to Step Seven.

STEP SEVEN

Humbly asked Him to remove our shortcomings.

Our work with Steps Four, Five, and Six—the searching, the admitting, and the making ready—put us in a position to relinquish self-will and experience the will of a Power greater than our own. We brought our freely-acknowledged faults to the God of our understanding and humbly *asked* to have them taken away.

Many of us misunderstood the meaning of humility. We may have thought it indicated weakness, submission, resignation, or compliance, but all of these imply we still had lurking reservations. Humility isn't weakness; it is strength. With humility we found total willingness to accept God's help. We were finally convinced that without it we could not achieve our goals. Humility gave us honesty and depth of vision—a realistic assessment of ourselves and our part in the scheme of things. It placed us in our true relationship with a Higher Power. Before all else, we stopped trying to control people and happenings in our daily experience. Our egos gave way to the Power in charge and the more we accepted that, the more we grew in the confident belief that there were other options open to us. We were no longer alone and we no longer felt helpless. We believed we could change and that all we had to do was *ask* for help.

When all went well, we tried to be grateful. When things went badly, we reminded ourselves there would always be events over which we had no control. How we reacted to these distresses was up to us. If we discovered new facets of our character that were not helpful to our recovery, we could turn again to our Higher Power. We did not need to fear our growing self-awareness because we could turn our thoughts to our spiritual source of help.

We could make this reaching out an ongoing process. It could be as continuous as our thoughts and feelings, acknowledging a sense of trust with each request. As our dependence on a Higher Power grew, we began to overcome the habit of relying only on ourselves. To rid ourselves of unwanted shortcomings, we learned to rely on assistance from a Power greater than ourselves.

It wasn't important how we asked for help—each of us found our own way to achieve this spiritual alliance. The importance lay in the act of asking. We acted on our commitment and because we believed we could be helped, we were. Renewed by surrendering our shortcomings, we were ready to move forward with our recovery and to meet life each day without the weight of yesterday's defeats.

Thinking It Over

As I go through the Steps and earnestly attempt to use them, I find the experience, strength, and hope of others who have taken the Steps before me. As I look into my own mirror, I can see who I really am—my strengths and my weaknesses. I don't have to be afraid to admit them to another human being. When I admit them to the God of my understanding, I place myself in the care of a Power that can release me from a course of excessive self-sacrifice or self-indulgence.

Now I am at a point where I can ask my Higher Power to take away my shortcomings. I can give them away and give in to a new reality. *Freedom from my old shortcomings offers me a new opportunity to learn better ways of thinking and doing. I can begin to concentrate on the qualities I would like to have in place of my shortcomings.*

I don't expect to reach perfection. What might such perfection mean? Since such a goal is beyond me, I will settle for the simple, reasonable one of getting comfortable with myself. Each day, each hour, I will do what I can to strive toward self-improvement.

A Step Seven Story

My first experience with Step Seven came after weeks of work on Steps Four through Six to honestly assess my shortcomings. My Higher Power and my Sponsor were unconditional in their love and support of me as I identified my behaviors, motivations, and attitudes that were harming me and others. When I felt I had been as honest as I was capable of being at the time, I transferred my list of shortcomings to a fragile piece of tissue paper. Then I drove to a state park where I have enjoyed many memorable experiences during my lifetime. I parked near the spillway at the end of the lake. As I looked out over the lake, I prayed that God would help me with this Step by removing my shortcomings. I folded the list into a tiny square, and I tossed it over the bridge into the water above the spillway. I was surprised at how quickly it disappeared. I felt a celebration in my heart that God was with me and that He was taking all the shortcomings that I was able to turn over to Him. Since that occasion, I have tried many times to fish out those shortcomings and make them fit again. Each time, God has reminded me that I am already done with them, and that I have already tossed them over the bridge because they do not serve me well.

I am grateful that Step Seven is not something I must finish, but as with all the Steps, may be worked again and again. Humility has a lot to do with faith and my belief in God's willingness to continue to work with me where I am. He patiently takes from me that which I am ready to let go of—sometimes over and over, as I take it back and have to let it go again. One of my greatest fears about Step Seven was that there would not be anything left of me when I gave up my shortcomings. When I let go, however, God showed me the behaviors, motivations, and attitudes that I wanted to nurture and grow within me.

As I stood on the bridge that day, I was letting go of old baggage that I no longer wanted to carry. Today my life is lighter and more joyful. This program has given me opportunities for growth that I never thought possible, and a relationship with a loving God that is rich and full, for which I am very grateful.

STEP EIGHT

Made a list of all persons we had harmed, and became willing to make amends to them all.

It was sometimes difficult for us to determine how something we had done could have hurt someone else or what hidden motives we might have had for what we had done. We may have even wondered why we should become willing to make amends.

We were asked to do something specific—take pencil in hand and write down the names of certain people.

Accepting this discipline with complete honesty may have caused us some pain. However, we found the result well worth it, for it presented the opportunity for us to have a clear conscience and gain a better understanding of ourselves. Taking this Step helped us begin to free ourselves of guilt. Although the guilt may have been deeply hidden in our subconscious, Step Eight gave us courage to bring it into the daylight. Later we could do whatever we felt necessary to free ourselves from the pain inflicted by our past actions. By doing our courageous best with this Step, we began to feel more comfortable with ourselves.

There were questions to ask ourselves in making our list: What did we do that hurt someone? Why did we do it? What were the consequences? Did it do permanent damage? Were there single instances in which we were unfair, unkind, deceitful, selfish, or hurtful? Or could we be putting too much weight on something that didn't really harm the other person?

One answer sufficed. If something we did in the past had left us with a feeling of gnawing guilt, then we added the name of the person we had hurt to our list. It was helpful to keep in mind the purpose of Step Eight, which was to relieve us of the painful and embarrassing memories that generated this guilt. Only by becoming willing to make amends in some way could we do this.

We may have been tempted to justify what we did by thinking, "But I did that only because of what she did to me," or "I really only meant to help him get sober. How could I know it was going to turn out that way?" We could not let ourselves take refuge in excuses, or Step Eight would not have done its best work for us.

We might have presumed that a wrong we did was due only to some character flaw in us, but this wasn't always so. Many of us did damage with beautiful qualities such as kindness, love, sympathy, and tolerance. Even with the best of intentions, we wreaked havoc on ourselves and others.

One area in which most of us found ample opportunity to put this Step into practice was in our family relationships. Here again, love and concern for husband, wife, children, or parents did not always assure we treated them well. Therefore we looked at our behavior to determine who belonged on our list.

The trials and stresses of living with an alcoholic certainly may have distorted our perspectives. If we had children, we carefully examined ways we may have harmed them, even unintentionally. Our over-protection might have deprived them of opportunities for growth. Loud, bitter quarrels may have done untold damage to youngsters by undermining their feelings of security and generating hatred for the alcoholic or others. Where such situations existed, we may have had many amends to make. Our children may have resented us the most because we were the non-drinking parents. If they heard angry reproaches or if we made them suffer for our frustrations, they may have felt even warmer toward the alcoholic. Our behavior may have seemed more irrational than the alcoholic's. We could take all these things into consideration when we made a list of those to whom we owed amends.

Finally, what about the harm we had inflicted on ourselves through the years? Hadn't we suffered because of our own errors of judgment, our willfulness, and other shortcomings? Most of us had many amends to make to ourselves now that we had found ways to improve our lives. Certainly we deserved to be on our list, too.

Thinking It Over

Taking Step Eight can help me dispose of many of my discomforts. It isn't that I will find total healing by making the effort to recall those I have harmed—perhaps even making the actual amends can't do that. Still I can feel relief as I acknowledge where I went wrong and hurt people.

When I think about the people I have hurt, I can look back to Step Four. Perhaps I overlooked some of my major shortcomings—the "hurting weapons" that led me to be unkind to people. I may realize, as I remember some of the things I have done, that I didn't put enough emphasis on those character flaws in Step Four. Now in Step Eight I can face them and become willing to make amends for everything those flaws led me to do.

I can list the names of those for whom I have shown a lack of concern and a total inability to feel how they were hurt by what I was saying and doing. I can ask my Higher Power to help me look at what I have done to others. If I want to be loved, I must learn to

love. Strange how the faults I was least able to acknowledge caused
me so much trouble. I hurt many people. I will try to put them all on
my list and pray for the willingness to make amends to them all.

A Step Eight Story

When I finished Step Seven, I was terrified of going on to Step
Eight. My Sponsor was insistent but very calm. She began to break
Step Eight into parts for me. First I wrote the list of those I had
harmed. I included almost everyone I knew, even myself.

My Sponsor told me to list anyone I felt uncomfortable about,
anyone I felt ashamed of my own behavior with, or anyone I would
cross the street to keep from meeting. It was a formidable list. She
also told me not to go on to the next part of Step Eight until I talked
with her. Since I knew I didn't have to go to Step Nine yet, I could
make a list.

After I made the list, I called my Sponsor. Then she told me to
write what happened that put each person on the list. I had always
made a production of everything, but she made this manageable by
limiting me to two sentences.

When I called to tell her that I had finished that part, she again
helped me manage the list. She told me to divide the list into four
groups: people I could make amends to quickly, ones who would be
harder to approach, ones who would be very difficult to deal with,
and ones to whom I felt I could never make amends. Just hearing
again that I didn't have to make amends *now* made me relax enough
to begin doing something. When the division was complete, I called
her again.

By the time I had gone through that list of people several times,
it was familiar. I had looked at each situation over and over. I was

still relieved that I didn't have to *do* anything yet, but I was sick of some of the situations hanging over my head. My Sponsor told me to pray for the willingness to make amends, but to talk with her before I made any amends that might make situations worse. She told me that while I was becoming willing, I could make living amends. I could change my behavior now so that I wouldn't have to work through Step Eight on the things happening today.

I will always be grateful for her detailed guidance on doing Step Eight. By doing this Step a little at a time, I was able to lose my fear and gain confidence that I could proceed to Step Nine—slowly and in God's time, not mine.

STEP NINE

Made direct amends to such people wherever possible, except when to do so would injure them or others.

Somebody once compared taking Step Nine to taking a dose of bitter medicine and then feeling wonderful afterward. It's an exacting Step, but taking it gave us practical, realistic ways to make amends.

A key word in this Step is "direct." This helped us avoid evading the issue when we were tempted to choose the kind of amends that would be the least painful or embarrassing to us. "Wherever possible" the amends were made directly to the person we had harmed. It was up to us to decide, with scrupulous honesty, whether making direct amends was possible or not.

Once we had made a list of those we had harmed, it was up to us to choose an appropriate way to make up for what we did. If it was something like thoughtless gossip or unkind criticism, perhaps a sincere apology might have helped. Often, however, this was not enough.

Frankly admitting we were wrong in what we said or did may have mended the breach. Therefore we decided to think over even minor situations before taking any step toward redressing a wrong. We found it wise to ask ourselves some questions before proceeding:

Would our amends open an old wound? Was this the right moment to make good for the hurt that we inflicted? Were we tempted to brush off our conduct because the person we offended was someone we didn't care much about anyway?

With the help of other Al-Anon members, we found that our likes and dislikes had nothing to do with our obligation to make amends. One of the reasons we took Step Nine was to gain peace of mind for ourselves by erasing our feelings of guilt. This was, in one sense, making amends to ourselves—not to be overlooked when working with Step Nine.

The problem was more difficult when something we did or said resulted in serious, perhaps irreversible, problems for others. These unkindnesses were usually harder to acknowledge, even after we brought them to the surface of our minds. However, it was necessary for our own peace of mind to review exactly what we did that caused the damage.

Perhaps we were too free with advice that, in the end, actually increased difficulties for the one we were trying to help. We might have been tempted to excuse ourselves by thinking, "I meant well, and anyway, he didn't have to take my advice." Such evasion still left us with the full weight of responsibility for making whatever amends were possible.

We found it crucial to face the painful consequences or injuries we caused so we could find real peace of mind. We also considered how our children were affected. All such matters were carefully examined and handled, because in trying to make amends, we didn't want to make things worse.

Many of us realized we owed important amends to that very alcoholic we once blamed for all our problems. Before we began to live by the Al-Anon program, it was difficult for us to admit we were at fault. Later we realized that we needed to face what we had done.

Whatever the outcome was from those years of living with alcoholism—whether sobriety, separation, or reunion—it was important for us to confront what we had done in bitterness and frustration. Here again, honesty and good judgment provided the key. Alcoholism brought dissension and misery to many relationships. Some of these could still be mended. We found many occasions in our daily lives when we could tactfully, maybe with a bit of humor, convey our regrets to the alcoholic, other family members, and our friends.

If direct amends could result in more hurt for others, we found other ways to make amends. We showed interest in another's well-being, activities, and achievements. Thoughtful courtesies suggested a basic change in our own attitudes and the way we behaved toward others. More gentleness, tolerance, and acceptance, along with our own sense of dignity, did much to restore harmony.

In other cases, we might have felt that amends were no longer possible. What if the person we had harmed was no longer alive or available to receive the amends we were longing to make? There was a comforting alternative: By being kind, thoughtful, and generous to those people currently in our lives, we could avoid repeating past mistakes. This was a form of amends we could make to those who were gone.

By taking these actions, we also found a concrete way to make amends for harm we may have done to ourselves. We learned to forgive ourselves as we realized that growth is a gradual process.

No matter what our relationships were or what actions we were contemplating in our attempts to fulfill Step Nine, a sincere effort to make good helped us find the most just and satisfying way to do it.

Thinking It Over

In working Step Nine, it is up to me to decide how its key words and phrases apply to my life. The important thing is to make amends, whether I am forgiven or not.

What form are my direct amends going to take in each case? Might I be tempted to sidestep when it would be embarrassing or humiliating to admit to the wrong I did? How can I be sure I wouldn't be lifting the lid of Pandora's box of troubles for somebody?

One thing is certain: this Step is a test of my honesty. Like the other Steps, it reminds me of the importance of humility. If I can successfully complete Step Nine, I will have brought myself to the threshold of the three spiritual Steps that follow it.

Although I am not entirely free of regret for past mistakes, I can foresee a welcome release from my uneasiness when I acknowledge the hurts I have inflicted on others.

Some amends to friends and relatives may seem too painful to make. One way might simply be to change my attitude toward these people and be less critical and more loving. Sometimes this is better than stirring up memories of past injuries which, if not too serious, may have been forgotten. A wholesome change in my way of behaving toward them can help me feel more comfortable with myself and my relationship with others.

I will review what I learned about myself when I was working on Step Four. Many of my wrongs against others grew out of the shortcomings I discovered in Step Four. If I was intolerant, it may have been caused by resentment. I might have been hurtful because of envy. Selfishness or greed may have led me to take unfair advantage of someone.

These realizations help me to understand how I came to hurt others. Making amends is still another step toward healing myself.

A Step Nine Story

My resentment of my alcoholic father was so great that he was not even on my first amends list. The effects of his drinking during my childhood were still impacting my adult life. Rarely a week went by without my anger surfacing. Sometimes I was not even aware of the anger until that snide remark rolled off my tongue.

As a child I was very confused, never knowing when my father would be on one of his periodic drinking binges. At an early age I learned not to bring friends home because his behavior was unpredictable. Yet when he wasn't drinking, Dad was full of love and laughter—really congenial.

As the disease progressed in my home, I isolated and escaped through reading. I had never heard the term "blackout" and could not comprehend that someone might not even remember doing or saying something. By the time my teen years ended, I had tried to commit suicide twice.

Years later in Al-Anon, working the Ninth Step with people on my amends list began to change my thinking about my part in relationships. At first I made direct amends, simply apologizing for any harm I had done them. Doing this brought a little relief and alleviated some anxiety. However, it did not change the dynamics of those relationships much. Later I learned that making amends was not just about saying I'm sorry, but rather about changing my actions and reactions. My behavior began to change when I consciously acknowledged my responsibility in each specific situation and worked through my Higher Power to change. Frequently my part had been one of omission and avoidance, so expressing myself was part of my amends.

Gradually my relationships changed, and I noticed that I felt more comfortable around my family and friends. I no longer had to pretend. I could take responsibility for my own feelings and allow others to do so, too. It was becoming easier to face conflict, and I was learning how to compromise. My world was becoming less all-or-nothing and more balanced.

When my father was diagnosed with dementia, my Sponsor gave me the nudge to clean up that resentment, too. This time, rather than a direct "I'm sorry" amends, I shared of myself. I took my parents out to dinner each week and listened to my dad share. As I listened, I began to remember the good times of my childhood and I realized that, indeed, I did love an alcoholic. I didn't have to remind him of any pain his drinking caused in my life. That knowledge would have only caused him harm and injured my own spirit.

Step Nine brought me freedom and love—freedom from lifelong anger and freedom to love and be loved. Step Nine encouraged me to participate in life. As a direct result of working this Step, I was able to be with my father, hold his hand, and say the Serenity Prayer just moments before he died. Today my memories of him are of a person who suffered from the disease of alcoholism. He loved and provided for me to the best of his ability. For that I am grateful.

STEP TEN

Continued to take personal inventory and when we were wrong promptly admitted it.

Each of the preceding Steps, especially Steps Four through Nine, helped prepare us for Step Ten. Through those Steps, we acknowledged the importance of recognizing our shortcomings and admitting them. We also realized that for the Twelve Steps to become a way of life for us, we would continue to observe and evaluate ourselves.

Our striving for fulfillment persisted as we taught ourselves to look for meaning and purpose in everything we did. It was less difficult if we made an honest effort to absorb and use the earlier Steps. We had already come a long way in the process of improving our lives. A continuing review became easier because of our earlier efforts. We had an ever-clearer picture of what we wanted to change. This self-knowledge came all the more readily when it was bolstered by our willingness to correct our mistakes as soon as they happened. Old habits of thought and actions became less automatic and compelling. Each time we overcame one, we received rich dividends in self-knowledge. When we came to recognize we had done something unwise, unkind, or ungenerous, we didn't feel quite easy until we had corrected the error.

There was a valuable bonus in devoting ourselves to Step Ten. It helped us realize that the errors we made hurt us. Surely none of us wanted our spiritual progress hampered by having unamended errors weighing on our conscience. We were not comfortable when we found ourselves in a situation we had created—and wished we hadn't. When we noticed we had reacted through selfishness, resentment, or any other fault, we realized these shortcomings were not entirely rooted out in our work with Steps Four through Seven. Lapses in our behavior hurt us, perhaps even more than they hurt others. However, they could also be lessons for growth. For this reason we kept ourselves alert to what we did and said. We promptly corrected whatever mistakes we made.

Thoughtful consideration convinced us that our views of a person or a situation were not necessarily infallible. If we could not accept the right of others to see things differently, we might have blundered into problems—those of our own making. Taking Step Ten gave us the opportunity to spare ourselves the consequences of being stubbornly opinionated. It reminded us that we were not all-wise, and that the philosophy of our Steps is based on humility—on acknowledging a Power greater than ourselves.

Step Ten asked us to continue to take action to wipe the slate clean and avoid building up regrets. Again we saw that the Al-Anon program was centered on us—on developing our own contentment with life. This led us to still another thought: not to allow ourselves to be affected or influenced by the demands and expectations of others. In our relationships with family and friends, we may have felt we were only trying to please when we did what someone else thought we should. We thought we were being unselfish when we put aside our own preferences and went along meekly with what somebody else wanted of us. What we were really doing was damaging ourselves. Perhaps we were afraid to refuse a request or demand. Maybe we were worried we would cross someone, especially if it was an alcoholic trying to manipulate and control us. In standing our ground we helped others realize that they could not impose their unreasonable behavior on us. We were properly protecting our own right to what was best for us. Being aware of that right served a dual, beneficial purpose and strengthened us to meet our difficulties with courage and confidence.

By working Step Ten, we observed what we did and why we did it. Examining our motives provided us with the tools to free ourselves of many problems that had troubled us in the past.

Thinking It Over

Step Ten can be a detailed method of fulfilling the ancient saying, "Know thyself." Would the self I want to know ever be uncaring, selfish, or condemning of others? If I feel there is something I ought to be sorry for, particularly if it resulted in hurting someone, I will not try to avoid my responsibility by thinking, "I was right in what I did," or "They deserved it." I will keep in mind that I was not assigned to judge others. My views, even those deeply ingrained in me, need not be applied to anyone else.

Whenever I decide I am in the wrong, I will be doing myself a good turn when I promptly admit it.

To think through the meaning of this Step and how I can best put it into action, I can ask myself the following questions:

- *Do I set aside a little time each day for thinking about myself, my feelings about the people I live with and meet, and my behavior toward them?*
- *Have I tried to be gentle and courteous toward others, especially those close to me?*
- *Do I keep in mind that the authority I have over my children should be used with love and tenderness? Do I realize that this can make them more responsive to my guidance?*

- *How do I feel when I let my temper explode and when I lash out at people without considering the consequences? Have I wondered what I look like in a mirror while this is going on?*
- *How do I feel when I learn that someone has made an unkind comment about me? How do I react? Do I ignore it? Do I lash out? Or do I try to forgive, knowing that I myself still have faults to overcome?*
- *What can I do to rid myself of personal prejudices about people I perceive to be different from me?*
- *Do I like myself better when I "Live and Let Live"?*

A Step Ten Story

The period just before I fall asleep seems the best time for me to take the Tenth Step. I find it easier to do it on a regular basis at the same time each day.

In taking a fearless and searching Fourth Step inventory, I didn't have to search too deeply to see the lengths to which I had gone to please people. I had reached the point where, if I talked to people and saw disapproval registered in their face, I would change what I was saying midstream and tell them what I thought they wanted to hear. As I worked on changing myself through the application of the Sixth and Seventh Steps, I started risking disfavor by being more honest. I began to tell people how I felt. It wasn't easy to allow others to see the anger or insecurity I had concealed for so long. I thought the whole world would see the real me with the volcano buried inside. They'd see that I wasn't the nice, sweet person who always had a smile and a kind word. The first time someone pushed in front of me in a line and I said, "Excuse me, I think I'm next," the words rang hollow in my ears as my face reddened. When

I told my husband I was keeping the dress he disliked, my heart dropped and my knees went weak as he stalked out of the room.

Several years passed. Expressing my real feelings almost became a habit, a regular part of my life. Standing up for my rights became easier with practice. Very often at night when I reviewed the day's happenings, I would congratulate myself for the tremendous strides I had made toward working on my defects and shortcomings of approval-seeking and people-pleasing. I marveled at my ability to say, "No." My husband, who balked at first, also commented positively on the change in my behavior. Spurred on by good feelings, I continued to assert myself more and more. There were times I didn't even recognize myself as the timid woman who had entered Al-Anon many years before.

Then after awhile, a feeling of discomfort returned. As I reviewed the day's happenings, I didn't feel as pleased with myself. Vague images and recollections flashed before me of daily scenes with shopkeepers, phone callers, friends, and members of my family. Was I being positive with that shoe salesman this afternoon or was I just being rude? Did I need to be so abrupt with that person on the telephone? Was I keeping that blouse that my husband didn't care for just to prove that he wasn't going to have his way? Suddenly it seemed that I had begun asserting myself to the point of defiance, even to the point of aggression.

One bone of contention between my husband and me concerned family gatherings. At first if he didn't want to go with me, I stayed home. Then I started to go alone. This worked for awhile; it was even an improvement. But the pendulum swung so far in the other direction that not only was I often unreasonable, many times I was cutting off my nose to spite my face. Though I desperately craved our togetherness on holidays, I was usually off and running by myself.

These realizations that came during my nightly spot-check, the Tenth Step inventory, didn't hit all at once. It was many nights of uneasy feelings, of thinking, "Something's not right; there's something I have to change," that brought the picture of the new me into focus.

Fortunately I was able to put balance back into my life before my new "assertiveness" became more of a character defect than the one I was trying to overcome. When I saw how I was acting, I was able to soften and change my behavior with people around me. I could also talk to my husband and explain what was happening.

I was also grateful that taking the Tenth Step helped me promptly admit I was wrong. This didn't come easily. Many nights I would find excuses for my behavior, but the constant application of this Step taught me how to say, "I made a mistake."

STEP ELEVEN

Sought through prayer and meditation to improve
our conscious contact with God **as we understood**
Him, *praying only for knowledge of His will for us*
and the power to carry that out.

If we had reason to be impressed with the helping Power of the earlier Steps, taking the Eleventh Step opened the door to new possibilities for many of us.

Study of its inner meaning brought many of us closer to a Power greater than ourselves. Each part of this Step had a way of enlightening us and giving us insight. We began seeing people, problems, and life in a new perspective. It was up to us to learn how we could best fit the Step to our needs. Each word and phrase reflected a particular idea. We sought to understand more clearly the part our own attitude played in determining what happened to us in our everyday life.

How did we do this? Through prayer and meditation. These were the means by which we learned to use our spiritual resources in solving our difficulties and making decisions, large and small. When we tried to find solutions in a purely analytical way by what we thought of as "figuring things out," the results were apt to be disappointing. We needed the help of a wisdom greater than our own.

The purpose of prayer and meditation was to improve our conscious contact with the God of our own understanding. Here the key word was "conscious." It meant making ourselves deeply, vividly aware of the Higher Power that has such a vital place in our lives.

The word "prayer," as a direct communication with that Power, appeared for the first time in Step Eleven. For some of us, prayer was our promise to surrender to God's will. When we were truly willing, it gave us confidence that our needs would be met in the best way for us. Step Eleven confirmed that prayer was asking only for "knowledge of His will for us," not for what we wanted or felt we deserved.

The word "meditation" simply meant concentrated thought on a chosen subject, considering it quietly, soberly, and deeply. Meditation denoted focusing all of our thoughts on something in order to understand it deeply. Perhaps it was serious and continued reflection or mental contemplation of a spiritual truth. As we meditated, we shut out all distractions and disturbing thoughts about problems and irritations. We brought our minds to bear on a single idea. It might have been a phrase, a thought from something we had heard or read, or a specific object we could picture in our minds.

It was not easy to fix our attention on one idea in this way. At first it took real effort to keep our thoughts from wandering to other topics or to revert to our daily trivia or decision-making. It was helpful, perhaps even necessary for some of us, to allot a specific time and place for our daily meditation. It was then that new insights were revealed to us.

Some of us were amazed to find an idea flashing into our minds that we'd never thought of before, along with the conviction that it was the right answer. Having received such unexpected guidance, we could also believe that we would be given "the power to carry that out."

Thinking It Over

I can begin to use the Eleventh Step with a good deal of assurance. With what I have learned in Al-Anon, I can try concentrating on the God of my understanding and let this Power guide me in all I do.

I want to let God into my life. I may stubbornly resist relating to or understanding a divine, universal, all-powerful idea.

I can sit quietly and become ready to communicate in confidence with the God of my understanding.

"Going it alone" for many years has brought me much trouble and frustration. One kind of deep trouble finally brought me to Al-Anon. I may have started out by embracing the idea that my Higher Power was my Al-Anon group—my friends who were doing so much to help me.

Little by little, I am able to accept the thought that my life has always been dependent on a Higher Power. As I gradually give up my willful denial, I may be able to feel a spiritual influence working in every part of my life. I can be brought to this realization by one word in the Eleventh Step: "improve." My conscious contact with God is far from complete; indeed, it may never be. It has to be improved continually, and the only way I can improve it is by sharpening my awareness of God's presence. Prayer and meditation are not just occasional activities to be done when I happen to think of them. They require a consistent, unswerving use of my thinking faculties to make myself more and more conscious of God's part in everything I think, say, and do.

As my effort becomes a daily exercise, I can feel my growing nearness to that Power so much greater than myself.

A Step Eleven Story

Before Al-Anon I had a religious upbringing and believed in God, but had no concept of His will for me. My prayers always gave Him requests, and I was repeatedly angry, frustrated, and disappointed at the results. I couldn't understand why He didn't answer my prayers. I felt unworthy, and after years of being unable to control my destiny and that of others in my life, I felt unloved. I never put God in the driver's seat. I thought prayer and meditation were one and the same. All these things were holding me back from improving my contact with God.

Through working the Steps in Al-Anon and listening at meetings and to my Sponsor, I have changed. My prayers are now for God's will in my life. I talk to Him of all the things that are important, both large and small, knowing that He is listening. I have learned to slide over and put Him in the driver's seat! The Steps gave me an awakening that I was worthy of love and forgiveness from God and others. I found that prayer is talking to my Higher Power. Meditation is that quiet time when I clear my head and find that calm, still place inside me where I listen for answers and direction. I receive a reservoir of inner peace and strength. The more time I spend in prayer and meditation, the more my relationship seems to develop with God. I am no longer obsessing or in turmoil over my life.

I make time for prayer every day, sometimes in different ways. I find a quiet spot where I can be alone. Sometimes it's in my yard by a bird feeder, near the garden, near a small stream or big lake, or at a park on a bench. Other times it's in my bedroom, at a table with a cup of coffee, or on a scenic drive in my car. I seem to feel closer to God when I am outdoors with nature and all its beauty. I have spent a lot of my life with an uncanny sense of restlessness, searching for something but not knowing what. I finally found it with this new way of praying to God. It is serenity.

It is important for me to remember the part of Step Eleven that says, "…improve our conscious contact with God *as we understood Him.*" It reminds me that we all have a different concept or view of God or a Higher Power and that's okay.

STEP TWELVE

Having had a spiritual awakening as the result of
these steps, we tried to carry this message to others,
and to practice these principles in all our affairs.

Here in Step Twelve comes the culmination of the spiritual nature of our shared experience. Whether we have realized it or not, we have had a rebirth of the spirit throughout our participation in Al-Anon.

It is the kind of spiritual rebirth that many of us have shared, and will continue to share in the future, as we absorb the inner meaning of the Twelve Steps and learn to live by them. We feel this can come about for others as it did for us when we devoted ourselves with all our hearts to the daily practice of these principles.

Have we had a spiritual awakening? Were we ready and willing to "carry this message to others"? Were we able to "practice these principles in all our affairs"? The words of this Step sum up many of the things we wanted in our search for a good life. We still feel that way.

We have come a long way from that first despairing time when we finally realized we had to let go of the problems that were overwhelming us. We were compelled to admit "we were powerless."

The Steps that followed were our re-education, changing the attitudes and reactions that grew out of our painful confusion. Taking these Steps gave us the confidence that came from relying on a Power greater than ourselves.

What could a spiritual awakening really do for us? It could set us free. It would not free us of problems; those we will always have as part of our human condition. Our release came from knowing that help was within our reach if we asked. This was the dependable way to get help, whether our difficulties came from living with alcoholism or any other situation in which we reacted in self-defeating ways.

Having studied and used the Steps, we can now say with confidence we have become better people. We have a clearer view of our problems and what we can do about them. This is a gift—a pattern for living that really works. It is our reward for the courage and determination we applied in using the Steps to change ourselves.

Also as a part of Step Twelve, we shall continue to try to carry this message to others. This was and is our opportunity to repay the good we received. Carrying the message to others has spread Al-Anon's help to troubled people all over the world. Every time, we fulfill that responsibility, our reward is an ever-richer gift.

We learned, too, the importance of gratitude. When we acknowledge what someone has done for us, our response makes all of us feel good. However, we found that real gratitude requires more from us than just returning the favor. It makes us want to offer kind and friendly service to others as well. Each day we find ample opportunity for this in our fellowship. There are so many lonely, confused, and troubled people who deserve to be comforted by our loving concern and our willingness to share the help we have received. We find it is not enough merely to attend meetings regularly, or even to accept a service position in the group. Carrying the message means personal one-to-one sharing with one another. It requires giving moral support by listening without criticism or condemnation to the troubles and misfortunes of another person. It means helping him or her to find the path we have found. In carrying the message, we share love and experience with the unhappy newcomer who blames others for everything that went wrong, just as we did before our eyes were opened. It means being willing to help the longtime member who sometimes finds it hard to apply the principles of the program to daily living.

Carrying the message does not mean solving problems for others. It means helping them solve their own difficulties without giving them advice that seems right to us but might not be right for them. Some of us found it difficult to think about others in this way, especially when we were beset with problems of our own. Yet avoiding this Twelfth Step work would have deprived us of valuable experience. Giving help makes us feel good about ourselves. Often sharing the burden of others also generates gratitude and love in them so they want to help others in turn.

Did we perhaps think we were too busy with our daily concerns to think about the needs of someone else? If we were self-conscious or timid, we may have found it difficult to open the door to communication. If we were receptive, however, people with problems were only too eager to ask for help. No matter what kept us from reaching out a helping hand, we could at least make an attempt. When we did, we discovered that we had done as much for ourselves as for someone else. An ancient philosopher put it this way: "There is no such thing as sacrifice. There is opportunity to serve, and he who overlooks it robs only himself."

We found our Twelfth Step continued with another thought: that practicing these principles in all our affairs could carry our effort still further. The principles are those guides that we discovered by taking the Steps. We were brought back once again to judge whatever we did, said, or even thought by the standards we had accepted through our work with the Twelve Steps. Many of us had to remind ourselves of the hazard of discouragement. We had a tendency to slip back into old habits and familiar faults. But we had only to look back to our beginnings in Al-Anon to reassure ourselves.

We never give up. We still continue to strive, one day at a time, to improve our lives by repeated practice of the Steps and all they imply. We follow Al-Anon principles each day to guard ourselves against confusion. The more closely our thoughts relate to a Power greater than ourselves, the more we find we are growing in humility, without which there can be no spiritual progress.

Thinking It Over

I can think of Step Twelve as a compact summary of our entire program. Its first statement intimates what I am working toward: a spiritual awakening. This awakening can increase my ability to see everything in life—people, things, and happenings—in a spiritual light. I can begin to see them in their relation to a Higher Power. Once I can reach that level, many things will become clear to me that never were before. I'll know instinctively what is right for me.

I can learn to share in meetings by learning about and experiencing God's love for me. In my gratitude, I can return that love to other people. I was selfish before Al-Anon. When I go to meetings, I can give encouragement to the new person. In making calls and in sponsoring newcomers, I can give patience and time. In every act of my Twelfth Step work, I'm giving—which simply means loving. In Al-Anon I have learned that I am loved just as I am. This gives me hope.

Carrying the message is a responsibility I have. I pray I'll always remember that in carrying the message to others, I do even more for myself than I do for them. Let me remind myself that what I do speaks louder than what I say.

I can work the Twelve Steps each day and practice these principles in all my affairs.

A Step Twelve Story

When I reached the Twelfth Step, once again I stumbled. Initially it seemed so simple: a sort of summing up of the first eleven Steps. I sighed with relief and ran to my Sponsor with the good news that I had done it. I was through. "Read it again," she said, as she had so often before. Gradually over the months three distinct parts of the Step came into focus.

Certainly I had hope for a dramatic spiritual awakening, as some of us have had. However, Step Twelve states this awakening would come as the result of practicing the first eleven. There was to be no easy shortcut—just hard work, with all the help I needed right at hand. Many times the going was slow; sometimes it was tedious; occasionally it was painful.

A few years ago, after I had been a member of Al-Anon for awhile, I literally turned my back on the spiritual power of this program. I still attended meetings, but was only "talking a good game." The hurt I caused my family and myself was and is very real. Nevertheless, this very Power that I had failed did not fail me. I received the tools to start again.

Now it is clear that, rather than experiencing one glorious moment, my growth will be gradual and ongoing.

So many people, in so many different ways, showed me the importance of carrying this message. Some shared in meetings or on a one-to-one basis. Others served at the group, district, area, or worldwide level. This service ensured that Al-Anon was there the day I went to my first meeting, and that it will be there for the newcomer tomorrow. This generosity enhanced my personal recovery and made the Steps come alive for me.

The truth of giving the program away in order to keep it was clearly shown to me when I offered to sponsor an Alateen group. I intended to give those young people what I had learned. Instead, they helped me laugh at myself and taught me a great deal about maturity. The Alateen members trusted me and proved it by their honesty. They showed me another facet of detachment—a lesson that proved invaluable in raising my own children. Finally I learned from them a great deal about what real love is. What priceless gifts. (And *I* was going to give to them!)

Taking the last part of this Step meant I could try to practice these principles in all my affairs. Having serenity is a snap sitting around a meeting table. It is much more challenging for me to attain around my family, friends, job, and with those people I know who "don't understand."

Having taken the Twelfth Step means I live these principles. When I admit to my neighbor or boss I'm wrong instead of rationalizing my behavior, I practice this program. When I forgive a hurt rather than hold a grudge, make the time to listen to my child, meditate, or anytime I'm really being good to myself, I am living the Al-Anon program. If I apply the Serenity Prayer to a trying situation, I'm the beneficiary.

I am nowhere near perfection and surely not yet done, as I once naively thought, but each day that I try to work this Step is good and getting better.

Part II

TWELVE TRADITIONS

TWELVE TRADITIONS

Our group experience suggests that the unity of the Al-Anon Family Groups depends upon our adherence to these Traditions:

1. Our common welfare should come first; personal progress for the greatest number depends upon unity.

2. For our group purpose there is but one authority—a loving God as He may express Himself in our group conscience. Our leaders are but trusted servants—they do not govern.

3. The relatives of alcoholics, when gathered together for mutual aid, may call themselves an Al-Anon Family Group, provided that, as a group, they have no other affiliation. The only requirement for membership is that there be a problem of alcoholism in a relative or friend.

4. Each group should be autonomous, except in matters affecting another group or Al-Anon or AA as a whole.

5. Each Al-Anon Family Group has but one purpose: to help families of alcoholics. We do this by practicing the Twelve Steps of AA *ourselves*, by encouraging and understanding our alcoholic relatives, and by welcoming and giving comfort to families of alcoholics.

6. Our Family Groups ought never endorse, finance or lend our name to any outside enterprise, lest problems of money, property and prestige divert us from our primary spiritual aim. Although a separate entity, we should always co-operate with Alcoholics Anonymous.

7. Every group ought to be fully self-supporting, declining outside contributions.

8. Al-Anon Twelfth Step work should remain forever non-professional, but our service centers may employ special workers.

9. Our groups, as such, ought never be organized; but we may create service boards or committees directly responsible to those they serve.

10. The Al-Anon Family Groups have no opinions on outside issues; hence our name ought never be drawn into public controversy.

11. Our public relations policy is based on attraction rather than promotion; we need always maintain personal anonymity at the level of press, radio, films, and TV. We need guard with special care the anonymity of all AA members.

12. Anonymity is the spiritual foundation of all our Traditions, ever reminding us to place principles above personalities.

AN OVERVIEW
OF THE
TWELVE TRADITIONS

Just as the Twelve Steps are designed for the personal and spiritual growth of those who are willing to follow the Al-Anon program, the Twelve Traditions are a pattern for the guidance of Al-Anon groups. They are as much a part of our spiritual foundation as the Steps. They describe the purpose of the group and suggest a design that will help it avoid distractions and errors that could dilute the program or confuse it with other entities.

Consider why some groups flourish and grow, while others with equally dedicated members stand still or even fall apart. Most often it depends on how well the members of the group understand and apply the Twelve Traditions.

Some of us might feel that our sole concern is with our personal problems, and therefore concentrate only on the Steps. We may not realize that the Traditions have anything to do with improving ourselves. We might also hesitate to ask the newcomer to take an interest in anything that doesn't apply directly to a personal problem.

Now that the problem of alcoholism is in the open, it has attracted widespread attention from the government, media, and professional counselors. This makes it all the more important for us to preserve the unique character of Al-Anon and the purpose of our groups. The fact that Al-Anon is a noncommercial, nonprofessional fellowship for those affected by someone else's drinking sets it apart from many other services and organizations.

What are the Traditions for? Why do we need them? The answer for both questions is the same: Al-Anon could never have worked so well for so many without this set of guidelines. The Traditions hold Al-Anon together, working for a common purpose and avoiding whatever might interfere with providing help for every member. They guide us in making decisions that protect the unique character of our fellowship. We turn to the Traditions whenever a problem arises, so we can find the solution that is best for all.

As we learn the meaning of the Traditions, we may want to incorporate them into our personal lives as well. These same principles that help us in preventing and resolving group problems can also be applied to many family and personal situations as guidelines to healthy relationships.

The Traditions are not rules. Accepting the guidance of the Traditions has been described as "obedience to the unenforceable." No one member of our fellowship has the authority to say, "You should not do this," or "You must do that." If a group fails to observe the Traditions, however, it risks the possibility of errors and conflicts that could deprive many troubled people of the help to be found in Al-Anon.

All of us can benefit from making ourselves familiar with the Traditions and how to apply them in the groups and in our personal lives. That is why many groups regularly read the Traditions at the opening of each meeting. In-depth study of individual Traditions can also be very beneficial.

TRADITION ONE

Our common welfare should come first; personal progress for the greatest number depends upon unity.

Every point made in each of the Twelve Traditions has a definite bearing on the unity upon which we all depend for help in Al-Anon. This unity is so vital to Al-Anon's existence that it is the focus of Tradition One.

Many of us come to Al-Anon to sober up an alcoholic. Others come to keep a sober alcoholic happy. Instead, we learn how to face the problems of living, or having lived, with alcoholism and how to correct the way we react to these problems. In doing so we learn a better way of life.

Our personal progress in this effort depends on the harmonious working together of all the group members. This requires a willingness to listen to the ideas of others with an open mind, sharing our views with them. We accept what the group's majority has agreed on, without insisting that our views be accepted. However, each of us has a responsibility to express those views.

Our progress also depends on sharing our experience, knowledge, and inspiration with others. We become willing to take on duties to serve the group and the fellowship—as Chairperson, Secretary, Treasurer, Group Representative, or in any other service role.

Our meetings are made up of talking and listening. Both are essential, but an extreme of either one can deprive others of help.

When we have something to share, we share it. However, when members use up limited meeting time to go on and on about personal grievances, they aren't helping anyone, including themselves. While we may have an urgent desire to unburden ourselves when troubles are weighing on our hearts and minds, that can be reserved for one-to-one talks, when the interchange is more likely to be helpful to both. That's one of the reasons for Sponsors, too!

On the other hand, a member who has gained valuable Al-Anon experience could try to withhold it at a meeting either out of shyness or a courteous wish to "let others talk." Those who habitually retreat into silence could deprive others of something they urgently need to hear. Something that is said aloud could also open the door to new, personal understanding. The strength of the Al-Anon program comes from recognition of our mutual needs. When we discuss them openly, we help ourselves and each other.

One important element in our unity is the use of Conference Approved Literature (CAL) in our group work. The Al-Anon message and the way it is delivered in our books and pamphlets is unique. The Conference Approval process assures that our literature represents the group conscience of our fellowship through actions taken by the World Service Conference. Our literature reflects the Al-Anon program in principle and practice. It is not diluted or distorted by differing points of view, which could be confusing and detrimental to the unity of our fellowship. It is essential for all of us, but especially important for newcomers, to "Keep It Simple" by concentrating on Al-Anon ideas as presented in our Conference Approved Literature.

Thinking It Over

Tradition One can open my eyes to my responsibility to my group. Since I really depend on Al-Anon to make life better for me, I will do everything I can to keep the group working for all of us as a whole.

Our common welfare and unity depend upon my willingness to agree to do what is best for the whole. This means, among other things, accepting the suggestions of the Traditions on such matters as outside therapies and organizations, and our determination to live within the financial means the members provide. It also means carefully preserving the anonymity of other members and concentrating on the program as explained in the Twelve Steps and our Conference Approved Literature.

Like others, I came to Al-Anon looking for ways to deal with problems related to the alcoholism of a family member or friend. I continue to go to Al-Anon to seek relief from pain and to find a new way of life as a part of a greater whole. I can achieve this best when there is a free and tolerant exchange of views and when all members understand how the Traditions serve to keep us united in purpose.

I know that the unity of worldwide Al-Anon, as well as the unity of our group, provides me with a core of stability I can depend on. If I am confused or upset, it is a good feeling to know I can rely on my group to give me comfort and reassurance. I also share the responsibility of safeguarding the group's welfare so it will be here when others need it.

A Tradition One Story

Maybe my experience, as painful as it was, will help somebody else overcome a big handicap—in the Al-Anon program as well as in life.

I have been a member of my group for five years. I have received a lot of help, but somehow I was never comfortable in the group. I stayed because there was no other one nearby. Despite my five years, I never felt I was accepted. There was always dissension about one thing or another, and I always felt I was the victim.

About a year ago, we got a new member. She'd had some years in Al-Anon but had only recently moved to our town. She and I seemed to click and we became friends. I told her about my difficulties with the group; I had an idea she sympathized with my complaints about the others. One day on an impulse I can't explain, I asked her to be my Sponsor. What an inspiration that was! Imagine a longtime member like me needing a Sponsor!

Some time later when we were having a heart-to-heart talk over lunch, she looked at me seriously and said, "Do you think you could take a shock?" "From you, anything!" I said cheerfully. Then she let me have it!

"Well, now, I've come to the conclusion, after long thought, that it's you who is creating the uneasiness in the group. Maybe you don't realize how strong-willed you are; I surely wouldn't have brought this up if I didn't love you." She went on, "I've wondered whether you'd ever taken your Fourth Step." I said I hadn't so we discussed it more.

Then she explained very carefully what she thought about the First Tradition, the importance of unity, and how one stubborn person could upset it. She reminded me how I'd contradicted others when they were speaking, and how I'd argued when somebody reminded me that we were not to bring in outside literature. She even reminded me of an occasion when I'd told a newcomer what to think.

I had to admit it all!

You might think this would have brought out anger and defensiveness, but with my Higher Power standing by me, my whole feeling was an overwhelming gratitude for this courageous help from my friend. She must have sensed that I was really ready.

I put my natural determination to constructive use by continuing to go to meetings and by learning to see myself as others saw me. I was ashamed and embarrassed, but finally happy to have that door opened for me.

Once I was able to remind myself I wasn't an all-wise authority on everything, I realized how much damage I had done to the unity of our group and to myself. Now I feel comfortable at meetings. I am accepting of others and feel accepted by them.

TRADITION TWO

For our group purpose there is but one author-
ity—a loving God as He may express Himself in
our group conscience. Our leaders are but trusted
servants—they do not govern.

Many groups have found themselves in predicaments because Tradition Two was not fully understood and observed. In Al-Anon there is no such thing as individual authority. All group decisions are arrived at through a majority agreement, reached after all elements of a situation have been considered. We call this agreement the "group conscience."

Our leaders are those who are willing to be servants—those who devote their time, work, and love to the fellowship. They have dedicated themselves to serving, not directing or controlling.

The Chairperson, Secretary, other volunteers in the group, those who serve at the area assembly, and the Delegates to the World Service Conference, as well as the Trustees, the committees, and employees at the World Service Office, are all leaders. They are also "but trusted servants." Such service does not give anyone authority over others. All do their best to serve, relying on guidance from their Higher Power. When a member has been appointed or elected to a specific office, it is simply an opportunity to serve and to carry out the responsibilities of that position.

Some members may have an inherent tendency to dominate everyone around them. Unless this tendency is self-checked through growth in Al-Anon, they may carry this behavior into the Al-Anon group. If this happens, the group can preserve the spirit of equality through the use of Tradition Two.

Often members of a group are only too willing to let their officers serve indefinitely. As long as someone else is willing to do the work, they do not volunteer to take over. These officers may gradually come to feel indispensable and important, and without realizing it, take managing attitudes. Sometimes one member after another leaves the group because of such management. Some simply join other groups, but others may give up on Al-Anon altogether, with no hope of finding the help they could have had in our program.

The work of the group should be shared. If the terms of service for each position are set in advance, it provides other members with the opportunity to serve, as well as to gain the experience such service gives.

Another source of difficulty can arise with sponsorship. It is important to make clear the distinction between guidance and advice. Guidance comes through sharing, listening, explaining the program, and pointing out choices available. Guidance never imposes a decision on someone else or dictates a course of action. The use of this Tradition will prevent a Sponsor from assuming authority over the member being sponsored; it offers protection to them both.

Al-Anon is a fellowship of equals. We are equally important, regardless of our social status, education, intellectual qualities, color, nationality, or religion. Al-Anon's door is open to anyone who really wants to learn how to live with problems caused by, or aggravated by, alcoholism in a relative or friend.

The fact that we are all equals encourages us to take an active part in the work of our fellowship, always with the purpose of serving and helping, never of controlling anyone else. This idea relates directly to a central theme of all our Steps and Traditions: humility. In Step Three, for example, this humility is described as our willingness to "turn our will and our lives over to the care of God *as we understood Him.*"

The progress of the members can be endangered when someone forgets that there is "but one authority." This authority is not an individual member, or even a clique that considers itself special. No one speaks for God—it is a loving God as expressed to each of us who forms our group conscience.

Thinking It Over

It is an interesting paradox that those Al-Anon members who study our program in depth and practice it faithfully in their daily lives are the "trusted servants" who have come to realize the spiritual essence of Tradition Two.

Using this principle helps the group when an occasional member thinks they know all the answers and tries to control the group or make independent decisions for it. Such a person may be motivated by good intentions, but behind it there may be the thought, "I know what's best." When an individual member assumes such authority, he or she prevents the others from the participation that is so vital to everyone's growth.

Our equality depends on realizing that our only authority is a loving God as expressed through our group conscience.

Tradition Two has an important message for me. Practicing it in my group as well as in my daily life will help me on my way to confidence and serenity.

A Tradition Two Story

Recently I attended an Al-Anon convention. On Saturday night, a group of us were having coffee with one of the convention speakers. Some of us were old friends, some new, but anyone would have felt at home, recognizing the laughter and sharing.

The conversation was general, until a member of my home group asked if I had attended a particular meeting in a neighboring town.

"Yes, I have," I answered, "and I'm never going to that meeting again."

"What happened?" asked someone.

"Well, I've gone there quite often and I used to enjoy it a lot," I replied. "It was really a great meeting but the last few months it's changed. Most of the members also belong to Alcoholics Anonymous. All they talk about is using the AA program to keep from drinking. I can get that at open AA meetings. I don't have a drinking problem, so there's just nothing there for me anymore. I'm not going back."

One or two others nodded in agreement; they had had the same experience.

Quietly the convention speaker said, "I know I'm not from around here and I don't want to interfere, but do you think you could go back just once more?"

My rather blunt reply was, "Why?"

"Well," she said, "it seems to me it's really concerned with the Traditions. I'm not sure; I think it's the Second. The members you're talking about must have come to Al-Anon for very different reasons than you're describing. After all, they were already active members of AA. There's a good chance they are unaware it has turned into a 'semi' AA meeting. Some of them may even be disappointed in Al-Anon without exactly knowing why. There's no reason you have to continue going to a meeting where you are uncomfortable. But if you don't tell that group why you are not going to attend anymore, are you being responsible? Aren't individuals who speak, even when they are in the minority, part of what group conscience is all about? Isn't that really how group conscience is formed?"

Someone else at the table interjected, "You've been in Al-Anon quite awhile, so you recognize when something is not quite right. You also know that there are other meetings, but what about the newcomer? Suppose it's someone's first meeting and they get the impression that the Al-Anon program is about ways to stop drinking? They may imagine that is great, or they may never go to another meeting anywhere again."

"I'll go with you," said a member who was also a member of AA. "Now I realize why I haven't gone back there. At first I thought that Al-Anon had nothing different for me, but don't misunderstand. AA gives me the gift of sobriety; I am first and foremost an AA member. But Al-Anon has given me the serenity to accept our daughter's drinking problem."

I thought for a minute and said, "Maybe nothing will change, but it is worth a try. And I used to think the Traditions were dull. We'll go back next Thursday. Wish us luck!"

TRADITION THREE

The relatives of alcoholics, when gathered together for mutual aid, may call themselves an Al-Anon Family Group, provided that, as a group, they have no other affiliation. The only requirement for membership is that there be a problem of alcoholism in a relative or friend.

This Tradition defines precisely what Al-Anon is and who is eligible to belong to an Al-Anon group. Yet its purpose and its limitations are not always understood.

It rarely happens that an Al-Anon group, as a whole, allows itself to be drawn into other affiliations. However, occasionally individual members might attempt to involve the group in other causes, therapies, religions, philosophies, or organizations. Sometimes groups invite speakers who may, in fact, be specialists in one helping profession or another, but who may not be familiar with the Al-Anon approach to the problem of alcoholism. Understanding Tradition Three prevents Al-Anon from becoming a ready-made audience for those who find it convenient or profitable to use our groups for other purposes. This Tradition helps us to guard against the confusion that results when we allow our program to be diluted.

Some of our groups have been invited to join others in outside activities, including retreats. Often these events are associated with specific religions, while Al-Anon is made up of people of many different beliefs. In Al-Anon spiritual discussions differ greatly from references to certain dogmas or creeds, which can lead to members feeling out-of-place. The phrase "no other affiliation" is one of the most important in all twelve of our Traditions. It tells us it is vital to devote ourselves to the study and practice of the philosophy that has helped so many others with problems such as ours.

This Tradition does not limit, in any way, what we choose to do as individuals. We are free to decide what other organizations we might join or where else we may seek help in solving our problems or searching for spiritual comfort. We are asked, however, not to dilute the Al-Anon program by discussing this outside help at our meetings.

This Tradition says, "The only requirement for membership is that there be a problem of alcoholism in a relative or friend." This simply means that anyone who fits that description may go to any Al-Anon meeting. Even if a group was formed with the intention of dealing with the specific problems of one category of persons, its meetings are open to anyone who is eligible to belong to Al-Anon.

Membership in Al-Anon is a personal decision. Individuals decide for themselves if they want Al-Anon and if they qualify for membership.

Some of us in Al-Anon are also members of Alcoholics Anonymous. The details of our struggle with alcoholism and our sobriety belong in our AA story and AA meetings. In Al-Anon we share how we have been affected by someone else's drinking. By focusing on our common experiences, we provide the mutual aid that is unique to Al-Anon.

Thinking It Over

There is something wonderfully reassuring about our Third Tradition. Although it is directed to the group, between the lines it tells me to focus my mind on the Al-Anon program. This fellowship can change my life for the better as long as I refuse to allow distractions to confuse me.

Tradition Three explains two ways in which I can "Keep It Simple." First I avoid being diverted from my program by outside influences. Second I welcome into Al-Anon anyone who feels they are or have been affected by someone else's drinking. Both of these are perfectly clear. They answer those who think it would help the group to concentrate on problems not related to alcoholism, as well as those who feel a newcomer should be rejected when, actually, he or she meets the only requirement for membership.

A Tradition Three Story

I moved here two years ago from another state where I had been active in Al-Anon. At one of the first meetings I went to here, I was told that my husband could never become sober unless he first attended a specific treatment center. My husband, however, was sober and had already been in AA for nearly two-and-a-half years. The Al-Anon members also spoke of how sick they all were and said it would take five years to get better. I felt fine, sane, and normal after two years of supportive Al-Anon meetings. I had never seen a time-limit for sanity and serenity in any Al-Anon literature.

At another meeting, I told a member how I felt about myself and my husband prior to Al-Anon. Before I could explain that I no longer felt that way, she told me that I needed to go to family therapy at the same treatment center. I told her I was finding my answers in Al-Anon.

At other meetings, I kept hearing terminology and phrases that were common to the treatment program but foreign to Al-Anon. In one instance, a newcomer was told that the only way to detach was to get a separation or a divorce.

We seemed to have two factions: those who wanted to adhere to the Traditions and keep Al-Anon Al-Anon; and those who wanted the Al-Anon meetings to be an extension of a treatment therapy that I felt lacked the compassion, love, and spirituality upon which Al-Anon is based.

Our local answering service often received calls from irate spouses who wanted to know why we had advised divorce. We were being mistaken for the treatment center. This was understandable since their philosophy had been expounded at our meetings.

At one such meeting, a newcomer was told that she, as well as her husband, had a progressive disease and she was either going to go crazy or die! She was given a choice: either she and her three children were to enter therapy, which they could not afford, or she should commit herself to a mental hospital. The poor woman was devastated. When she called me, she planned to have herself committed. I talked to her three times that day and once the next morning. Then I took her to one of the few remaining meetings in the area I knew to be truly practicing the Al-Anon program.

Things worked out well for this member, but I wonder how many others there are just like her who don't know anyone to call.

TRADITION FOUR

Each group should be autonomous, except in matters affecting another group or Al-Anon or AA as a whole.

This Tradition gives our groups freedom in all essential matters. Every group is free to choose its own meeting program and topics for discussion. It can decide when and where it meets, if and when it will have open meetings, who will speak at them, and how its funds will be distributed. This freedom, however, also carries a responsibility for preserving the unity of Al-Anon throughout the world.

Every group and every member is trusted to protect and preserve the character of our fellowship. The Traditions themselves provide our guidance. A group that keeps itself familiar with them is not likely to make decisions that would damage any part of the fellowship. We are also all responsible, as groups and members, for presenting a favorable picture of Al-Anon to the world at large. By following our Traditions, we ensure that Al-Anon will be all the more appealing to those who need our help.

Now let's consider some of the actions that cannot be justified by group autonomy:

Sometimes someone will happen on an idea that seems appealing but overlooks the fact that we're all part of a united fellowship. From time to time, members have decided to rewrite the Twelve

Steps and distribute them to local groups, causing great misunderstanding and confusion.

At some meetings, members have introduced literature that has not been Conference Approved. In the early days of our fellowship when only a few pieces of literature were available, some groups produced and distributed their own leaflets. As Al-Anon grew, it became important for our written message to be consistent with the principles of the program.

Therefore in the early 1960s, the World Service Conference agreed that all Al-Anon literature should be Conference Approved. One by one, the early productions dropped out, and our literature is now published only by the World Service Office, with every piece submitted to the process for developing Conference Approved Literature. If any segment of the Al-Anon fellowship were to issue or use literature that had not been Conference Approved, it would clearly damage the unity of the fellowship as a whole. A unified message in our literature is the glue that holds Al-Anon together.

On the other hand, it is within group autonomy, for instance, to decide how to open and close our meetings, keeping in mind the impact that it may have on Al-Anon, Alateen, or AA as a whole. Some groups start with a moment of silence followed by the Serenity Prayer. Others include the Preamble, Suggested Welcome, the Twelve Steps, the Twelve Traditions, or the Twelve Concepts of Service. There is just as much variety in the way meetings are ended. Some use the Suggested Closing, along with the Al-Anon Declaration, the Serenity Prayer, the Lord's Prayer, or another spiritual moment of the group's choosing. The choices are many and wide.

Any autonomous action of the group, however, is measured by its effect on another group, or Al-Anon, or AA as a whole.

Thinking It Over

This Tradition helps me see that every decision my group makes could be tested by the question, "Is this good for our fellowship?" Sometimes groups have ideas that they feel could put our message across to more people who need it. They have the responsibility to make sure these ideas don't have consequences that would be more prudent to avoid.

A Tradition Four Story

Just as we finished dinner, the phone rang. When I answered, it turned out to be a call from the fourth person who was very unhappy about what had happened in a group in our district.

It seemed that, for three weeks in a row, outside speakers had been invited to address the meeting. One had outlined his method for treating alcoholics in a newly-opened counseling office. On another night, a couple explained how they worked with couples. During a third meeting, a woman told about family therapy at the agency where she was employed.

Each person who phoned was understandably very upset. Some had attended all of the meetings, some only one, but each had expected it to be Al-Anon and each was disappointed. The opportunity for shared experience, strength, and hope had been lost. There was no way to undo what had happened.

While it was clearly within the group's prerogative to make program decisions, this was an instance where it also affected the fellowship as a whole. Not only had members wanted an Al-Anon meeting and been disappointed, but what about members from other groups who attended those nights? And newcomers, expecting to be introduced to Al-Anon, could be confused by what seemed to be a showcase for professional therapies.

Because I did not belong to this group, the best I could do was to remind the callers that there was a great deal each of them could do to ensure that something such as this wouldn't happen again.

First of all, they could, as individuals, express their feelings to the group's Steering Committee and to the whole group. They could also become more active in their group and participate in decisions about future meeting topics. They could suggest that group experience had shown it was better to have outside speakers at other than regular meeting times. Finally, they could point out that more concern be given in planning open meetings.

I hoped the group members would realize autonomy also carried the responsibility to follow our program. After hanging up the phone, I quietly said the Serenity Prayer and went on to wash the dishes.

TRADITION FIVE

*Each Al-Anon Family Group has but one purpose:
to help families of alcoholics. We do this by practicing the Twelve Steps of AA* ourselves, *by encouraging and understanding our alcoholic relatives,
and by welcoming and giving comfort to families
of alcoholics.*

As many of us have learned from applying the Twelve Steps to
our lives, the spiritual basis of the Al-Anon program is universally
applicable. These Steps, which we borrowed from AA and adapted
to our own needs, are also being used by other support groups and
organizations.

People sometimes ask why our groups don't broaden our focus
to help those who are trying to cope with another's addiction to
drugs, gambling, or other problems. Why do we limit ourselves to
alcoholism when alcohol is a drug and gambling a compulsion?
The ultimate success of Al-Anon and its members depends on
focusing ourselves on our one purpose: helping the families and
friends of alcoholics.

Tradition Five suggests that we will best be able to help others
when we ourselves practice the Twelve Steps. They give us guidance for sharing with each other by giving comfort and, above all,
by learning to listen. For each of us, it is a relief to be able to talk
freely with someone who understands.

Helping the families of alcoholics also means guarding against anything that might defeat our purpose, including gossip. If someone tells us about personal family matters, are we careful not to repeat anything told to us? Do those we sponsor, or newcomers, feel they can safely bring us their secrets in moments of crisis, when they so desperately need someone to talk to and trust?

It may be easier for us to see ways of helping "families of alcoholics" than to accept the idea of "encouraging and understanding our alcoholic relatives." Before Al-Anon the alcoholic may have been the target of our bitterness and anger. We may have thought it was the drinker who was to blame for everything that went wrong in the family. It may never have occurred to us that this troublesome human being would need or deserve our compassion. Thus we are challenged by this Tradition to learn about the disease of alcoholism. Giving encouragement and understanding to this person will help us with our recovery.

We welcome the families and friends of alcoholics any time we share our experiences. We give comfort when we listen with concern, offer our friendship, and assist newcomers as they learn to help themselves. In these ways, we communicate that Al-Anon is a safe place to overcome the isolation and despair that many of us suffered when dealing with an alcoholic.

What does this Tradition say to those of us who are willing to carry out the three actions it suggests? It says that Al-Anon is a loving program. By showing concern for other people, we can free ourselves from bitterness, resentment, and the anguish of repeated defeats. Understanding and accepting alcoholism as a disease can give us compassion for the alcoholic's suffering and can help bring about our own serenity and spiritual growth.

Tradition Five is made up of ideas so constructive and helpful that it can make a big difference in our lives.

Thinking It Over

Tradition Five seems to have three special messages for me. Those messages concern "giving comfort" to people in trouble. I can use the Steps to gain spiritual and emotional comfort for myself. I can gain understanding of the disease of alcoholism and cooperate in the alcoholic's recovery. I can also help others like myself.

Much of my progress in the program comes from learning to welcome every opportunity to respond to someone in need of understanding, comfort, and patient, uncritical listening.

When I have times of loneliness, even forlornness, I can avail myself of such comfort from other members. I can also provide a willing ear and a kind word to those around me. Often this helps me concentrate less on my problems. As I begin to reap the rewards, working this Tradition will become easier and more satisfying.

A Tradition Five Story

Some years ago, our group had a new member who not only was seeking the spiritual help that Al-Anon can give, but was in obvious need of financial assistance.

She was young, with five small children. Her husband, because of his alcoholism, was unable to provide his family with adequate food, clothing, and shelter. One night she came to the meeting in tears. There was no food in the house and the children had been without milk for three days. At the time, the group had about $60 in the treasury. I suggested we give her $30 of the group's funds to show our love and concern.

We were about to do this when a more experienced member shared that Tradition Five explains the specific ways we help the families of alcoholics. They do not include offering financial help. Attempts to do this could divert the group from our primary spiritual goals. We decided not to use the group's funds.

As I've gained experience in Al-Anon, the wisdom of the group's decision is even clearer to me. Over the years, many members—longtimer and newcomer alike—have had serious personal financial difficulties. If we tried to meet these problems with group money, we would have failed miserably. Instead, we provided help through spiritual support. Rather than limit us, this Tradition channels our efforts to the areas where we can be most effective.

We cannot make alcoholics sober, but we can help the families and friends of alcoholics retain their sanity and ability to function. We cannot meet others' financial needs, but we can provide the comfort mentioned in Tradition Five by sharing our experience, strength, and hope. Our own spiritual needs can be fulfilled as long as we do not try to do things that will divert us from our primary spiritual aim.

TRADITION SIX

Our Family Groups ought never endorse, finance or lend our name to any outside enterprise, lest problems of money, property and prestige divert us from our primary spiritual aim. Although a separate entity, we should always co-operate with Alcoholics Anonymous.

A crucial phrase in the Sixth Tradition is "never endorse, finance or lend our name to any outside enterprise." This idea has always been important in preserving our integrity. It is just as essential today because of the tendency for people in other organizations to want to use Al-Anon to advertise or promote their theories and therapies.

The Al-Anon program is designed to help a particular group of people. As individuals we may support, financially or otherwise, any other activity—religious, political, academic, charitable, or whatever else our interests suggest. Although we may have much in common with other causes, endorsing or supporting them as a group could lead to misunderstanding and confusion.

Halfway houses for abused spouses or clubhouses for recovering alcoholics and their families might appeal to many of us as projects worthy of support. Yet if an Al-Anon group were to become involved in the management of such enterprises, it would certainly become involved in matters beyond our purpose. This could also leave little time for concentration on our program, thereby diverting "us from our primary spiritual aim."

In keeping with this Tradition, Al-Anon does not endorse films or literature produced by other organizations, no matter how good they may be.

This Tradition also speaks of cooperation with Alcoholics Anonymous. This does not mean giving financial support or forming combined Alcoholics Anonymous/Al-Anon groups. To serve its membership, a group is either Al-Anon or AA. Each group has a different purpose, so a group cannot be both. On the other hand, some Al-Anon groups periodically plan joint open meetings with an AA group. An occasional talk by an AA member at an open Al-Anon meeting can be interesting and helpful. If we are invited to speak at an open AA meeting, we tell our own stories, not the alcoholic's. We emphasize how Al-Anon has helped our own recovery from the family disease of alcoholism.

There are many ways for us to cooperate with AA that help us both achieve our "primary spiritual aim." When both fellowships participate in a convention, there are suggested guidelines to assure cooperation. Large conventions require considerable advance planning. Those interested in having the other fellowship participate can begin by inviting a liaison member to attend planning sessions. Each fellowship should be responsible for its own agenda, speakers, and activities, while the host would be responsible for the overall plans, renting the facility, etc.

Another area in which Al-Anon and AA may cooperate is where Al-Anon has not grown sufficiently to support its own Al-Anon information service office or intergroup. It may share facilities with AA, provided that Al-Anon meets its portion of the financial expenses (desk space, telephone, etc.) and is responsible for handling all Al-Anon Twelve Step calls. When Al-Anon grows strong enough to support its own office, separate facilities from AA are desirable.

Thinking It Over

Tradition Six is very important in protecting Al-Anon's identity and preserving its unity. Now I can resist the desire to solve all the world's problems or the temptation to get my Al-Anon group's support for any number of worthwhile projects. I have learned the hard way that diversions cause disunity and controversy.

Various professional therapists and writers have many opinions on what to do about alcoholism and the alcoholic. When our members add one or more such ideas to our meetings, they divert us from the practice of a program that works. I can keep my own opinions about these ideas without referring to them in my Al-Anon meetings. The study and practice of our Steps and Traditions is the way to serenity.

I am grateful to AA for the principles of this program, but I also realize that our separateness is our mutual strength.

A Tradition Six Story

So often in life I feel bombarded by politics, technology, religion, and other outside interests. It comforts me to know that when I attend an Al-Anon meeting, the only ideas I will hear and discuss relate to Al-Anon. Bringing various causes into an Al-Anon meeting could imply that as a fellowship we endorse or support them, which could bring Al-Anon's credibility into question. It is a relief to know that these topics are left outside the door. We don't discuss Alcoholics Anonymous topics in Al-Anon either, but it's nice to know that we have respect for and cooperate with AA.

I also apply Tradition Six to my personal life, in that often issues of money, property, and prestige can divert me from my primary purpose—which is my spiritual growth and recovery. An only child, I grew up in a "nice-nice" family. I attended the right private school, took the right extracurricular classes, and said the right things. Money, property, and prestige were what made our family who we were. To show any signs of imperfection to the outside world was a conspiracy against our fine name. *What would people think?* Inside our house, my family constantly bickered and my home life was chaotic and unpredictable. My father was an alcoholic and workaholic. My mother reacted to his behavior by stuffing her anger and playing the sacrificial victim. My parents were my first teachers about life and how to cope with it. I had so many things to unlearn, and I moved far away from them to do it.

Today I try to be aware of how money, property, and prestige can play a role in my character flaws. *What* I do or do not have is not related to *who* I am. *How* I look outside may not reveal *what* I feel inside.

Currently, we are moving to be closer to my parents, who have aged and are both very ill. They still live in the same town where I grew up. Their flaws have only been amplified with time. Today, I feel nothing but compassion for them just as I would for someone suffering from emphysema. I do what I can to help without jeopardizing my own health or my obligations to my own family.

At first, I felt I had to have the biggest house we could afford, regardless of the quality of schools. I was going to prove to people that I had made it, that I was okay now! Then my husband reminded me that bigger may not be better and isn't required for *our family's* happiness.

I realized that I hadn't included God or my family in this house search; I had only thought of myself. I continually prayed for my Higher Power's guidance.

We have found a smaller, older home in an older neighborhood where the schools are better. It is absolutely charming and fills all of *our* (not just my) needs. I still have a lot to unlearn and relearn. I have little control or concern over what other people think. Regardless of where I live or what I do or don't have, it's who I am and my relationship with God that counts. Because of Al-Anon, I have learned to stay out of managing any other person's recovery and instead focus on my own.

TRADITION SEVEN

Every group ought to be fully self-supporting, declining outside contributions.

Our financial pattern is simplicity itself, yet questions do sometimes arise that need to be clarified.

According to Tradition Six, money contributed to a group by its members is not to be used for "outside enterprises." This money is for Al-Anon purposes alone.

Here in Tradition Seven, we see the other side of the coin: where a group's money comes from. The main source is the contributions members drop into the basket when it is passed at each meeting. There are no dues or fees but, as part of a greater whole, each group takes responsibility for supporting local, national, and worldwide Al-Anon services (our "service arms"). Each group is free to decide how much it can afford to contribute to each of these activities. Most of our groups are willing to provide whatever they can, since every Al-Anon member shares in the benefits of this support.

Contributions by members at their regular meetings are usually adequate to meet these needs. Occasionally, however, a group will hold a fundraiser within the group to raise extra money. For those groups that still have a surplus after supporting their service arms, there is always an opportunity to carry the message by buying literature for distribution to institutions, churches, schools, doctors' offices, and elsewhere.

In keeping with this Tradition, the membership supports the

World Service Office by means of contributions by individual members and groups, donations from area conventions, and the sale of Conference Approved Literature. Members support the work of their World Service Office, area, and local services. In turn these service arms are responsible to the members they serve. This interdependence is a wholesome and sustaining condition preserving all Al-Anon in unity and equality.

The last part of the Seventh Tradition refers to "declining outside contributions." This applies to the groups as well as to the World Service Office, our key to worldwide unity. Accepting outside donations would change the entire structure of the Al-Anon fellowship and destroy its basic spiritual foundation.

In the past, many offers of financial support have been received from non-members who thought we were doing something worthwhile. Was it ungracious to refuse these donations? No, because we realized such offers could carry expectations with them. If accepted, we might feel obliged to make concessions to the donors. Even in a small way, it would mean selling a bit of our independence. To keep Al-Anon free of outside influence, we look to ourselves for support.

It is also important to remember that the self-support referred to in Tradition Seven includes not only our money, but our time and energy. No matter how much money we contribute, Al-Anon's survival depends equally on our willingness to provide service in whatever way possible.

Thinking It Over

In the simplest terms, this Tradition points out one of the cornerstones of the Al-Anon program of recovery. When individual members and groups understand that they are responsible for their own survival and progress, a great spiritual strength flows into each part as well as the whole. If I do my part and others do theirs, we do it together, and we don't need to ask someone else to do it for us.

A Tradition Seven Story

Our local information service recently received a letter from the director of a nearby facility for the rehabilitation of alcoholics, with a check enclosed. The letter read in part:

"We decided to contribute $150 toward your superb work. Many of our staff have become acquainted with the Al-Anon Family Groups during their work here. We have both admiration and appreciation for the help you are giving to the families of alcoholics. May the best of God's blessings continue to be yours as you invest your time and talents in the healing of others."

That gracious gift would certainly have been difficult to refuse if it wasn't for our Tradition Seven. How easy it could be to fall into the trap of evaluating agencies or favoring one facility over another because we felt indebted to it. Our answer read in part:

"Thank you very much for your interest in Al-Anon Family Groups. While we are most grateful for your generosity, we cannot accept the check you sent because Al-Anon is self-supporting according to its Traditions. We are delighted to hear that many of you have found Al-Anon useful and we hope you will continue to suggest how valuable our program can be to families who are suffering."*

---

*Some service arms also notify the facility that as an alternative they may purchase subscriptions to *The Forum* magazine or Al-Anon Conference Approved Literature and materials with the money they planned to donate to Al-Anon. This literature can then be given to families and friends of the facility's clients. This action would fall within our Traditions and help us carry the message about our program to those who could use its help.

TRADITION EIGHT

Al-Anon Twelfth Step work should remain forever non-professional, but our service centers may employ special workers.

An integral part of Al-Anon is Twelfth Step work. Each member helps others in need of the comfort and new approach to living that Al-Anon can provide. The reward of such work is the joy of sharing what we have found in this fellowship. There is nothing professional in any of this. What we do for others is not done for money or any other material gain, but only to further our own spiritual growth.

Providing Al-Anon's service to so many troubled people around the world is our major responsibility. In the groups, no matter how many or how large they became through the years, Al-Anon service has remained nonprofessional. Our major purpose is to foster an opportunity for a loving interchange of help and encouragement through personal contact. So it is today, with many thousands of groups in many lands, speaking many languages, and embracing many different beliefs.

Tradition Eight provides guidance to the members who happen to be professionals, including counselors, lawyers, clergy, medical personnel, and social workers. It encourages them to keep their sharing in meetings on a personal basis, with their own recovery as their primary concern. They do not attend Al-Anon meetings in their professional capacity, as experts in the field of alcoholism, or to solicit clients.

The second part of Tradition Eight says, "our service centers may employ special workers." When Al-Anon was new and our cofounders started the original "Clearing House," volunteers did the office chores, letterwriting, record-keeping, and housecleaning. As we grew, we needed a full-time staff for the ever-growing tasks of this central office. Therefore we hired and paid experienced workers for the work they did.

Today, in such a large and far-reaching fellowship as ours, the work of the World Service Office requires business organization. This not only assures orderly procedures and maximum production, but fulfills the requirements of state and federal laws. Workers with various skills are needed, including accountants, secretaries, and many other specially-trained people, who are not necessarily Al-Anon members. However, certain World Service Office staff, trained in particular aspects of service, are always Al-Anon members. Like the World Service Office, service centers throughout the world may also employ special workers.

Thinking It Over

The more I learn about Tradition Eight, the more valuable it becomes to me. It is important for my group to keep the line sharply drawn between Al-Anon and outside influences. Some of our members have taken extensive training to become professional counselors. Other members may be familiar with the jargon or methods of the counseling they have received. The Eighth Tradition reminds me to keep Al-Anon free of alteration or dilution.

Professionals who join Al-Anon do so for their personal recovery. Tradition Eight restates a basic principle of our program: We have no authority figures. To recover, we meet as equals. By sharing personal experiences, strengths, and hopes, we help one another.

A Tradition Eight Story

In growing up and in my chosen career, my life had always revolved around professionals. How could nonprofessionals ever help me? That seemed impossible until I came to Al-Anon. It wasn't until I had some personal experiences in testing this Tradition that I realized its validity. Perhaps its truth lay more importantly in how I hindered my own recovery than in the harm that I did to Al-Anon. When I tried to mix professionalism into my own program it didn't work.

When I first had contact with the program, I latched onto it as the answer to all my problems. Here was a place where the difficulties of the alcoholic family were really understood. I realized that all those wonderful people had experienced the same suffering I had and could empathize with my pain. No one gave advice. There were only suggestions from the experiences of individuals who had used the tools of the program and found that they worked.

As I began to feel better, I wanted to help others, too. With all my years of postgraduate schooling and training, I felt well qualified—even though none of that training ever worked for me!

When I started helping people, I was flooded with phone calls from other Al-Anon members. Most of my responses must have sounded more like consultations than Twelfth Step calls. Although many members seemed grateful for my help and benefited from it, something began to happen to me. I lost the program. I was helping as a "professional" and I went downhill—badly. I became depressed and hopeless. I had stopped using the program for my own recovery.

Finally I had reached a bottom lower than any I thought possible. Then I made a telephone call in desperation —a call to help myself. A dear, loving, understanding member gently suggested that I come back to the program—for me.

Since then, many good things have happened. I am a professional, working in the field of alcoholism. I owe a great deal of my success to my own recovery in Al-Anon—recovery I need to continue as a member of the fellowship. When I go to meetings, I go to get help for myself and to share my feelings and growth with others. The Al-Anon program pervades every area of my life. While at work, I suggest participation in Al-Anon to families and friends of alcoholics, but I do not expound on the program. I go to Al-Anon meetings as a member of the fellowship, not as a professional. I can "Let It Begin with Me."

TRADITION NINE

Our groups, as such, ought never be organized;
but we may create service boards or committees
directly responsible to those they serve.

In most organizations, people at various levels have the authority to direct the activity of others. A fellowship of equals, such as
ours, doesn't work that way. In an Al-Anon group, no one may
give orders or expect obedience of anyone. We get our necessary
work done by the use of spiritual principles and logical procedures
agreed upon by everyone involved.

True, a group does elect or appoint individual members to take
care of various chores—a Program Chairperson, Secretary, Treasurer,
Group Representative, or any other necessary group officer. These
trusted servants are responsible to perform faithfully the positions
they have accepted. Using group funds, they help provide refresh-
ments, buy Al-Anon literature, or pay rent for the meeting place.
According to the decisions reached by group conscience and in line
with our Traditions, they plan meetings, lead meetings, take care of
finances, and keep members informed about Al-Anon events and matters of interest. Officers are rotated on a regular basis. No one stays
long in any position so that all have a chance to share responsibility.

All members have an opportunity to serve the group and the fellowship. This does not include a right to direct or control the other
members.

While the groups only require minimal structure, our service arms must be sufficiently organized to work effectively. The "service boards or committees" mentioned in Tradition Nine include the following service arms: information services, central offices of an area, area assemblies, and the World Service Office, which is the clearinghouse for all the Al-Anon Family Groups. These service arms have committees or boards that deal with specific areas of the overall work. They may also have salaried employees who carry on the day-to-day functions. Although they exercise no authority over the groups they serve, they do listen to and carry out the voice of the fellowship as expressed in the group conscience.

Thinking It Over

My understanding of the meaning of Tradition Nine changes as I grow in understanding of our fellowship. At first it may seem to me that a group must have rigid structure to avoid chaos. Later I might feel the Tradition means that officers are not needed at all. Neither extreme works well. Filling certain positions gives form to the meeting. Rotating officers guarantees that all members have a chance to grow through service.

I am in Al-Anon for my own recovery. By volunteering to serve in various capacities, I translate into action such sayings as "Let It Begin with Me."

A Tradition Nine Story

A letter to the World Service Office outlined a group problem. It is one that has occurred over the years in one form or another in other groups:

"The five members who started our group two years ago consider themselves to be the 'Charter Members.' They have drawn up a set of rules and regulations that they say we must follow. They enforce a no-smoking ban, call the roll at each meeting, record minutes, and also close the business meeting to everyone they don't consider to be members of our group. They even have a sign that says 'KEEP OUT.'

"We have a lot of disharmony. At present, the 'Charter Members' are deciding who they will ask to leave the group. One member has been told she cannot attend because work makes her arrive late. Can the World Service Office help us?"

The answer from the World Service Office read in part:

"Tradition Nine cautions us about groups being organized. The term 'Charter Member' is not used in Al-Anon because those who begin groups turn over leadership to newer members as soon as possible. Then everyone in the group has an opportunity to serve and grow.

"Business meetings are conducted in several ways. Some groups hold a business meeting during their regular meeting. Others hold one before or after the regular meeting so program time is not taken up with business. A number of groups prefer having a Steering Committee, which is usually made up of the present officers. This is not a decision-making body. Its function is to suggest matters to all the members so that a vote can be taken. This is how a group conscience decision is reached.

"Perhaps the group will consider reading the Traditions before their meeting. It might also be helpful to take a group inventory."

TRADITION TEN

The Al-Anon Family Groups have no opinion on outside issues; hence our name ought never be drawn into public controversy.

Tradition Ten goes further than Tradition Six in confirming, once more, the purpose of all our Traditions—to keep ourselves, as a group and a fellowship, clear of anything not related to our program.

Those of us who are involved in other causes may be tempted to share them with the group by bringing them up in group discussions or as topics for talks. Within the fellowship, the one thing that has brought us together must remain our sole concern. Otherwise it could lead to controversy, not only within the group but on the public level.

Tradition Ten suggests that Al-Anon should not take a stand for or against any public issues or social causes, however important they may be to members as individuals. Such involvement could lead Al-Anon into public controversy, which might seriously affect our unity and continued growth.

We are a fellowship of many thousands of members from many backgrounds, races, religions, and nationalities. We have a wide variety of viewpoints. Taking a position on any outside issue would surely divide us from within. A free, unbiased, uncontroversial atmosphere in which to develop belongs to all. Individual Al-Anon members carrying the message at the public level do not express opinions on outside issues; Al-Anon, as a fellowship, has none.

Suppose an Al-Anon group were to become actively involved in an outside project—even one that may seem akin to our common bond, such as supporting legislation for funding the rehabilitation of alcoholics. Even if we were able to have all the members of the group agree, there might be other Al-Anon groups with differing views and solutions. Given any worthy cause, each approach to the problem may be different and result in division. Supporting any outside cause diverts us from our primary spiritual aim. If we pursue one worthy cause, what would keep us from pursuing others?

While Tradition Ten refers specifically to controversy on outside issues, many members feel the spirit of this Tradition makes controversy of any kind an unwelcome guest at Al-Anon meetings. Members coming from the hostile atmospheres that often prevail with alcoholism may be discouraged by controversy at meetings. Each of us has been wounded by the effects of this disease in our lives. We come to the Al-Anon meeting seeking comfort and understanding, free from dissension. We are free to have our own opinion, but we strive to do so without angry disputes.

By avoiding anger and controversy, Al-Anon members of differing political and ideological beliefs have been able to come together at meetings and share their experience in dealing with alcoholism in an atmosphere of mutual respect. In Al-Anon we can concentrate on our common bond rather than on our differing views on outside issues.

Thinking It Over

This Tradition emphasizes avoiding anything that would lead to public controversy. Am I tempted in a meeting to speak out against some social or political situation or to encourage others to declare their opinions? If so, I will concentrate instead on the Al-Anon program.

I am personally responsible to do my part to ensure that Al-Anon does not become involved in any question that could focus public attention on my group as part of some political, social, or religious cause. Such activities distract us from our primary purpose and discourage potential newcomers from attending Al-Anon meetings.

Tradition Ten reminds me again of Al-Anon's one purpose: to help families and friends of alcoholics. As a service to myself, to my friends in the fellowship, and to Al-Anon as a whole, I will avoid doing anything that would link the Al-Anon name with any public controversy.

A Tradition Ten Story

Some years ago, a series of articles appeared in a local paper in our state. The author attacked the not-for-profit status of Al-Anon and accused the fellowship of soliciting funds from the general public and not accounting for their use. The author went further, demanding an investigation of Al-Anon by the State Attorney General.

Quite a few of our local members sent copies of the articles to the World Service Office suggesting that it was the responsibility of the office to refute these claims in a letter to the editor.

While it was a natural reaction for the members to want to respond, Tradition Ten kept Al-Anon from becoming involved in a public controversy. Neither the author nor the paper was directly contacted by the World Service Office. Pertinent records were supplied to the Attorney General at his request. The documentation made it apparent that the charges were false. The Al-Anon name was cleared without having to offer a public denial.

TRADITION ELEVEN

Our public relations policy is based on attraction rather than promotion; we need always maintain personal anonymity at the level of press, radio, films, and TV. We need guard with special care the anonymity of all AA members.

When Tradition Eleven was drafted, the words "public relations" had a broader connotation. In more recent years, this term has been associated with commercial, profit-making, or fundraising organizations. The motivation of such organizations is different from Al-Anon's. For this reason, we now use the more definitive terms "public information" or "public outreach" in our literature to describe our efforts to let people know about Al-Anon. Rather than promoting, we're trying to attract and comfort those whose unhappiness and confusion we understand so well. We want others to know that friendship and help are waiting for families and friends of alcoholics in an Al-Anon group.

Over the years, the media has increasingly recognized Al-Anon and its work. This recognition has brought many newcomers into Al-Anon. Often a single unsolicited mention by media representatives has brought inquiries from thousands of people in search of help.

Giving information about our fellowship has been important from the earliest days. In a sense, every one of us is a medium of public information and public outreach. In spreading the message, discretion must be our watchword. The Tradition specifies that anonymity be maintained when we appear in the media. We remain anonymous in publications, radio, film, television, or the Internet to keep our egos in check. This is a direct confirmation of a theme of our Steps and Traditions—humility. If members promote their association with Al-Anon and build a personal following, it gives a distorted picture of the nature of our fellowship.

On the other hand, there are members who misinterpret this Tradition. They keep their association with Al-Anon so secret that they miss many opportunities to share its help with those in need. Members doing public outreach or serving in a specific office, such as Area Delegate, give up a certain measure of their personal anonymity, since they are the contacts with outside agencies as well as within the fellowship. This is still within the Eleventh Tradition, since it does not break anonymity in the media.

The last sentence of Tradition Eleven refers to the anonymity of all AA members. It suggests that, in all situations, we do not reveal the full name of anyone in AA.

In the final analysis, we want everyone to know about Al-Anon's availability. Tradition Eleven gives us guidance on how to accomplish this.

Thinking It Over

This Tradition is another strong reminder of the emphasis our Twelve Steps and Twelve Traditions place on humility. In stressing personal anonymity in the media, Tradition Eleven helps me keep in mind that Al-Anon is a fellowship of equals. Every member can be just as much a representative of the program as I am.

Provided I don't reveal my full face or full name in the media, I can attract potential members to our program. Beyond that, however, my anonymity—or lack of it—is my own personal decision. While it is important that I not reveal other members of the program, I am free to let family, friends, and the professional community know what Al-Anon is and how it can help.

A Tradition Eleven Story

I was a Chairperson of an Al-Anon intergroup in the capital city of a large country, where Al-Anon had been trying for some years to develop a workable structure to unify the widely scattered existing groups. One day we were approached by a national TV station to tape an interview about our program. It was a wonderful opportunity to carry the message. Three other members and I participated in the taping. In the course of this, we appeared full face to the camera and proudly gave our full names. We also explained that our husbands were all AA members. They had given us their permission for this disclosure.

The same evening, the intergroup was hosting a large meeting with several Al-Anon members who had come from another country to share their experiences with us. Immediately after I announced at the meeting that this taping was soon to be broadcast, one of our visitors pointed out that to divulge complete names with full face to camera and identify ourselves as Al-Anon members and wives of AA members was contrary to the spirit of the Eleventh Tradition. It could prove most damaging to the healthy growth of Al-Anon by distorting the basic principle of anonymity, a cornerstone of our fellowship.

Fortunately it was possible to contact the TV station the following day and they agreed to withhold the tape and do another interview in which we appeared as Al-Anon members, using first names only and with our backs to the camera. The program was subsequently broadcast nationally and brought many new members into the fellowship, reassuring them that their anonymity would not be endangered.

TRADITION TWELVE

Anonymity is the spiritual foundation of all our Traditions, ever reminding us to place principles above personalities.

In Al-Anon one of our greatest gifts is the privilege of helping others find their way from despair to hope. We help others and keep ourselves open to being helped. There is no room in this important purpose for self-glorification and pride. There is much room for gratitude, humility, and willingness to serve.

The same theme runs through our Steps as well, beginning with the word "powerless" in the First Step. The power we have comes from a Higher Power and not from our own wisdom and virtue. This is directly stated when we are reminded to place principles above personalities.

The Twelfth Tradition reaffirms the principles of all our Traditions. When we act and think as members of Al-Anon, we are able once more to see that our will alone does not determine the reality of a situation.

When we subordinate our will to the spiritual strength of the group, unity adds to the healing process. When we do not emphasize our uniqueness, we gain strength from being part of a group conscience that flows from a Power greater than ours alone. When we leave our other affiliations outside Al-Anon's doors and recognize the common problem that brings us together, we often feel for the first time in our lives that we are where we belong.

Through this sense of belonging we realize we are responsible for our own recovery and measure it in spiritual terms. Eventually we realize that this Tradition has within it the basis for change that can lead to solutions of personal, family, and group problems. Our spiritual growth through humility has its roots in the principle of anonymity.

Thinking It Over

Placing principles above personalities, as Tradition Twelve suggests, presents a paradox. Throughout my study of the program, I am reminded to be aware of what I am doing, how I am reacting to others, and what I can do to improve myself and my life. This surely means thinking of myself a great deal. Won't this make me self-centered? Won't it keep me from caring about other people and their needs? As long as I remember the principles I am asked to follow in Al-Anon and use them as a yardstick in what I do and how I relate to others, this will not happen. Although I still have a long way to go, these principles can help me fulfill my potential.

A Tradition Twelve Story

Since attending Al-Anon, there are several lessons I have learned that come to mind when I think of anonymity and the spiritual idea behind "principles above personalities."

The first lesson occurred during my early Al-Anon days. During that time, my attitude was one of many curious contradictions. There I was, full of fears and insecurities. At the same time, I was such a snob. I sat at meetings in judgment of others. I decided that certain members who made a good appearance and seemed intelligent had something to offer. I concluded that others couldn't possibly have anything of interest to say to me. It's ironic that one of the people I disregarded because of poor grammar was later to become my Sponsor.

My next difficulty with Tradition Twelve came about because I placed trust in other people—trust that I should have reserved for my Higher Power. Completely defeated by alcoholism, I gave the alcoholic such control over my life that I had no other Higher Power. Next I transferred this dependency to other Al-Anon members. These were several well-spoken members with winning personalities that I admired. When they said something was so, I took it as truth. How shattered I was when I learned that some of my idols were human, and how unfair it was for me to put them on pedestals. I had to learn that the only one who deserved that kind of blind faith was my Higher Power.

My third lesson, and one that I still struggle with, is not to allow my personal knowledge about a member to interfere with what they say. For example, there was a member of my group who had wonderful words of wisdom about detachment that I needed to hear. Knowing her personally, I took her inventory and unfortunately concluded, "Why should I listen to her? She's not doing such a great job with her own detachment." When I recognized my distorted thinking, I asked myself, "Who am I to judge how another person works the program?" Today I try to remember the words my Sponsor passed on to me, "Don't discount the message just because you don't like the messenger."

The way I see it now, what happens within a group transcends the individual. As I observe this spiritual principle of anonymity and the more willing I am to learn from everyone, the more able I am to decide what is appropriate for me.

EPILOGUE

In Al-Anon, we are united by a single, simple, spiritual program. A letter from one member said in part:

"I often think of a picture that came to my mind when I first read the Twelfth Step and tried to understand it. I looked back on my troubled life before Al-Anon, when I felt as though I were groping around in a terrifying dark cave. No matter how desperately I prayed and struggled, I felt trapped. There seemed no way out of the hopeless confusion of my life.

"Suddenly someone—a stranger—took me by the hand and led me around a turn in the cave that opened up into a tunnel, dotted by a row of lights. He led me as far as the first light and said, 'Just keep following the lights and you'll be all right.' I didn't care where they led as long as I could get out of the deep despair where I was living.

"As I walked from one light to the next, the path through the tunnel became brighter and brighter and my fears gradually faded. Finally there came the brightest light of all—sunshine and freedom!

"The lights were our Twelve Steps and our Twelve Traditions, which kept showing me the way out of my confusion. With them I felt wholly secure.

"I knew there were many others like me who couldn't find their way to that tunnel lighted with lamps of hope. Remembering my own pain, I tried to start many others on the path to that ultimate sunshine we find in our beautiful program."

TWELVE CONCEPTS OF SERVICE

The Twelve Steps and Traditions are guides for personal growth and group unity. The Twelve Concepts are guides for service. They show how Twelfth Step work can be done on a broad scale and how members of a World Service Office can relate to each other and to the groups, through a World Service Conference, to spread Al-Anon's message worldwide.

1. The ultimate responsibility and authority for Al-Anon world services belongs to the Al-Anon groups.
2. The Al-Anon Family Groups have delegated complete administrative and operational authority to their Conference and its service arms.
3. The right of decision makes effective leadership possible.
4. Participation is the key to harmony.
5. The rights of appeal and petition protect minorities and insure that they be heard.
6. The Conference acknowledges the primary administrative responsibility of the Trustees.
7. The Trustees have legal rights while the rights of the Conference are traditional.
8. The Board of Trustees delegates full authority for routine management of Al-Anon Headquarters to its executive committees.

9. Good personal leadership at all service levels is a necessity. In the field of world service the Board of Trustees assumes the primary leadership.
10. Service responsibility is balanced by carefully defined service authority and double-headed management is avoided.
11. The World Service Office is composed of selected committees, executives and staff members.
12. The spiritual foundation for Al-Anon's world services is contained in the General Warranties of the Conference, Article 12 of the Charter.

GENERAL WARRANTIES
OF THE CONFERENCE

In all proceedings the World Service Conference of Al-Anon shall observe the spirit of the Traditions:

1. that only sufficient operating funds, including an ample reserve, be its prudent financial principle;
2. that no Conference member shall be placed in unqualified authority over other members;
3. that all decisions be reached by discussion vote and whenever possible by unanimity;
4. that no Conference action ever be personally punitive or an incitement to public controversy;
5. that though the Conference serves Al-Anon it shall never perform any act of government; and that like the fellowship of Al-Anon Family Groups which it serves, it shall always remain democratic in thought and action.

INDEX

A

AA *see* Alcoholics Anonymous

Acceptance 5, 8, 13, 21-22, 25, 28, 34, 37, 39-40, 49, 57, 62, 69-71, 85, 88-89, 95, 136

Admitting

    powerlessness 7-11

    wrongs 31-37, 61-66

Affiliations 97-100, 135

Al-Anon 95, 97-100, 120-121, 141

    as a fellowship ix, xi-xii, 74, 83-84, 91-93, 101-104, 109-113, 115-117, 119-122, 123-125, 127-130, 131-134

    as a way of life ix-x, 9, 33, 61, 85, 87

    focus 98

    history xi-xii

    meetings xi-xii, 8, 74, 76, 78, 84, 89, 101-102, 111, 115, 119, 122-125, 128, 137

    open meetings 101, 104, 110

    program ix, xi, 13, 76, 78, 83, 86, 91-95, 99, 105, 109-113, 120-122, 127, 139

    purpose ix-x, 83-84, 87, 91, 105-108, 115, 129, 135

    separate entity 109-113

    see also Affiliations, Authority, Autonomy, Concepts of Service, Leaders, Membership, Name, Principles of Al-Anon program, Public relations policy, Steps, Traditions, Unity

Alateen xi-xii, 78

Alcohol 7-11

Alcoholics 51, 56-57, 59-60, 85, 97-100, 103, 105-108, 117

Alcoholics Anonymous (AA) xi-xii, 11, 18, 94-95, 98, 99,
    101-102, 109-111, 131-134
Alcoholism
    as a disease ix-x, xi-xii, 8, 27, 57, 74, 83-84, 87, 92, 97-100,
        119, 122
    as a family illness/disease xii, 105-107
Amends 49-53, 55-60
Anger 10, 14, 47, 50-51, 58, 89, 106, 128
Anne B., cofounder of Al-Anon xi
Anonymity 87, 131-134, 135-137
Attitudes 9, 15, 22, 26, 34, 36, 47, 57, 58, 67, 137
Authority 91-95, 123-124, 141-142
Autonomy 101-104

B
Behavior 14, 25-29, 64, 78, 92
Bitterness 33, 50, 51, 57, 106
Blame 27, 39-40, 43, 56, 75, 106
"Bottom," reaching 122

C
Carrying the message 73-78, 103, 115, 127-128, 131, 133
Change 16, 20, 28, 92, 98-99, 104
    basis for 136
    changing ourselves xi, 9, 13-14, 19, 25, 41, 45, 57, 58,
        61-66, 73
Children xi-xii, 14, 50-51, 56, 63, 78, 100, 107
Comforting families of alcoholics 87, 105-108
Common welfare 85-89
Concepts of Service ix, 102, 141-142
Conference Approved Literature (CAL) 86-87, 102, 115-116
Controversy 61-66, 127-130

D

Defects of character 26-27, 32, 39-44, 61-66
    see also Harm, Injuring others, Shortcomings, Wrongs
Divert from spiritual aim 108, 109-113

E

Encouragement 76, 93, 105-108, 119

F

Family 50, 62-66, 77-78, 84, 98, 105-108, 122, 129, 136
Fear 8, 14, 29, 46, 48, 52-53, 137, 139
Films 110, 131-134
Finance 87, 107-108, 109-113, 115-117, 123
Friends/friendships ix, 3, 26-28, 33-36, 78, 97-100, 106, 122,
    129, 131

G

God of our understanding ix, 10, 15-17, 19-24, 31-37, 39-44,
    45-48, 67-71, 76, 93, 112-113
    see also Higher Power, Power greater than ourselves
Group conscience 91-95, 104, 108, 125, 135, 141-142
    see also Inventory, group
Growth 8-9, 15, 20, 77

H

Harm 49-53, 121
    see also Defects of character, Injuring others, Shortcomings,
      Wrongs
Higher Power 13-25, 31-32, 39-44, 45-48, 67-71, 76, 89, 91, 112,
    135, 137
    see also God, Power greater than ourselves
Humility 14, 31-37, 45-48, 58, 62, 76, 93, 131-134

I

Information service/intergroup 110, 115, 133
Injuring others 55-60
    see also Defects of character, Harm, Shortcomings, Wrongs
Inventory
    group 91-95, 104, 108, 125, 135
    personal 25-29, 61-66, 137

J

Jargon 100, 120, 125

L

Leaders 91-95, 123-124, 141-142
Lists
    of shortcomings 27, 33, 35-36, 47
    of persons we've harmed 49-53, 55, 59
Literature 99, 102, 110, 115-116
Lois W., cofounder of Al-Anon xi
Love 21, 27, 37, 47-48, 50-52, 59-60, 63, 70, 74-78, 88, 91-95,
    100, 106-107, 119, 122, 133

M

Meditation 6, 67-71, 78
Membership 97-100
Money 107-108, 109-113, 115-117
Mutual aid 97-100

N

Name
    Al-Anon xi, 109-113
    Members' 133, 134
Newcomers 16, 20, 75, 78, 83, 88, 89, 95, 99-100, 103, 106-107,
    131-134

O

Obedience to the unenforceable 84
Opportunity 75
Organizing 123-125
Outside enterprises 103, 109-113, 115
Outside issues 127-130

P

Power greater than ourselves ix, 5, 13-18, 15, 19-24, 31,39-44,
     45-48, 62, 67, 74, 76, 133, 135
     see also God, Higher Power
Powerlessness 7-11, 31, 135
Prayer 6, 15, 67-71
Prestige 109-113
Principles of Al-Anon program 6, 73-78, 135-137
Problems 62, 67, 73-75, 83-84, 104, 122-125, 136
     of alcoholism 97-100, 135
     of money/property/prestige 109-113
Professionals 83-84, 103-104, 119-122
Program *see* Al-Anon program, Principles of Al-Anon program
Progress 85-89
Promptness, in admitting wrongs 61-66
Public relations policy 109-113, 131-134

R

Readiness 39-44
Relatives
     alcoholic ix, 105-108
     of alcoholics 97-100
     see also Alcoholics, Alcoholism, Family, Friends/friendship
Responsibility
     group 123-125
     personal 7, 39, 60

S

Sanity 13-18, 99, 108

Self-knowledge 9, 33, 43, 46, 61, 63

Self-supporting 115-117

Serenity Prayer vii, 60, 78, 102, 104

Service arms 115, 116, 117, 123-124, 141

Shortcomings 5, 25, 27, 31-37, 45-48
    see also Defects of character, Harm, Injuring others,
        Wrongs

Slogans
    "Keep It Simple" 18, 99
    "Let Go and Let God" 9
    "Let It Begin with Me" 124
    "Live and Let Live" 9, 66
    "One Day at a Time" 76

Special workers 119-122, 120

Spirituality ix, 14-15, 20-21, 34, 41, 46, 62, 68-69, 93, 98, 100,
    105, 107-108, 116, 123, 139
    spiritual aim of Al-Anon 109-113, 128
    spiritual awakening 73-78
    spiritual foundation of Traditions 83, 135-137, 142
    spiritual growth 6, 83, 106, 119, 136

Sponsorship 29, 34, 36, 47, 52-53, 60, 70, 76, 77, 86, 88, 92,
    106, 137

Steps
    in general 3, 39-41, 83, 93, 101-102, 132, 135, 139, 141
    history of xi-xii
    Step One 7-11
    Step Two 13-18
    Step Three 19-24
    Step Four 25-29
    Step Five 31-37
    Step Six 39-44

Step Seven 45-48
Step Eight 49-53
Step Nine 55-60
Step Ten 61-66
Step Eleven 67-71
Step Twelve 73-78
Suggested Preamble to the Twelve Steps v, 2

T

Three Legacies ix
Traditions
    in general 81-82, 83-84, 93, 100, 102, 111
    history of xi-xii
    Tradition One 85-89
    Tradition Two 91-95
    Tradition Three 97-100
    Tradition Four 101-104
    Tradition Five 105-108
    Tradition Six 109-113
    Tradition Seven 115-117
    Tradition Eight 119-122
    Tradition Nine 123-125
    Tradition Ten 127-130
    Tradition Eleven 131-134
    Tradition Twelve 135-137
Trusted servants 91-95, 123-125, 141-142
Turning it over 19-24, 31
Twelfth Step work 76, 78, 119-122

U

Understanding
    of God *as we understood Him* 19-24, 67

of our alcoholic relatives 105-108
Unity ix-xi, 81-82, 85-89, 101-103, 111, 115-116, 127, 135, 141
Unmanageability 7-11

W

Warranties, General 142
Welfare, common 85-89
Will
    God's will 67-71
    our will 19-24
World Service Conference 86, 91, 102, 141-142
World Service Office 91, 102, 116, 120, 124-125, 129
Wrongs 31-37, 50, 51, 61-66
    see also Defects of character, Harm, Injuring others,
        Shortcomings

٢